CALLED TO COMMUNITY

New Directions in Unitarian Universalist Ministry

DOROTHY MAY EMERSON
AND
ANITA FARBER-ROBERTSON

CONTRIBUTIONS BY
MARY MCKINNON GANZ
REBECCA ANN PARKER
KATHLEEN R. PARKER

ISBN: 1484149831

ISBN 13: 9781484149836

Library of Congress Control Number: 2013908089

CreateSpace Independent Publishing Platform
North Charleston, South Carolina

CALLED TO COMMUNITY

New Directions in Unitarian Universalist Ministry

PRINCIPLES AND PURPOSES OF THE UNITARIAN UNIVERSALIST ASSOCIATION

We, the member congregations of the Unitarian Universalist Association, covenant to affirm and promote:

- The inherent worth and dignity of every person;
- Justice, equity, and compassion in human relations;
- Acceptance of one another and encouragement to spiritual growth in our congregations;
- A free and responsible search for truth and meaning;
- The right of conscience and the use of the democratic process within our congregations and in society at large;
- The goal of world community with peace, liberty, and justice for all;
- Respect for the interdependent web of all existence of which we are a part.

The Living Tradition we share draws from many sources:

- Direct experience of that transcending mystery and wonder, affirmed in all cultures, which moves us to a renewal of the spirit and an openness to the forces that create and uphold life;
- Words and deeds of prophetic women and men which challenge us to confront powers and structures of evil with justice, compassion, and the transforming power of love;
- Wisdom from the world's religions which inspires us in our ethical and spiritual life;
- Jewish and Christian teachings which call us to respond to God's love by loving our neighbors as ourselves;
- Humanist teachings which counsel us to heed the guidance of reason and the results of science and warn us against idolatries of the mind and spirit;
- Spiritual teachings of Earth-centered traditions which celebrate the sacred circle of life and instruct us to live in harmony with the rhythms of nature.

Grateful for the religious pluralism which enriches and ennobles our faith, we are inspired to deepen our understanding, and expand our vision. As free congregations we enter into this covenant, promising to one another our mutual trust and support.

Bylaw adopted by the Unitarian Universalist General Assemblies 1984, 1985, and 1995

PROCLAMATION OF THE SOCIETY FOR THE LARGER MINISTRY

We, as people living in a world that is both dying and seeking to be reborn, who are shaken to our very roots by the massiveness and depth of planetary and human suffering, are empowered by a driving passion to bear witness to that suffering, participate in its transformation, and affirm the inherent glory of life.

Therefore, we do covenant together:

- To respond to these cries of pain, to our own brokenness, and to awaken the healing spirit of hope.
- To engage in a broad spectrum of ministries through and with Unitarian Universalist congregations, with the larger community, and increasingly, in a global context.
- To celebrate the diversity of life within our elemental interconnectedness.
- To challenge one another as individuals and as members of institutions to identify, analyze, and act upon the basic causes of human hurt and separation.

Thus empowered, we join hands with the community of faith in acknowledging the larger ministry which addresses our common vision. We call upon our denomination to recognize a variety of lay and ordained ministries as embodiments of the Unitarian Universalist principle and purpose. All of our creative ministries including academic, administrative, aesthetic, AIDS, campus, camp and conference centers, chaplaincies, community-focused, environmental, gay/lesbian/bisexual, healing, legal, men-focused, music, parish, pastoral counseling, pastoral psychotherapy, peace, religious education, social justice, women focused, young adult and ministries not yet envisioned . . . are valid, necessary, and life affirming.

Such compassionate, liberating, prophetic ministries are at the very heart of our religious tradition.

This document, signed in November 1988 by thirty-seven founders of the first community ministry organization, is accepted as a founding document by the Unitarian Universalist Society for Community Ministries.

TABLE OF CONTENTS

FOREWORD

Documents that give voice to movements for needed change provide an irreplaceable record of the inspiration and passion that motivated all who made it happen. This book—which makes known the vision, effort, frustration, and joy that brought community ministry into a place of greater prominence and recognition in Unitarian Universalism—is such a record.

My first conversation with Dorothy Emerson was in 2004, when I agreed to research and write a chapter on the history of community ministry among Unitarians, Universalists, and Unitarian Universalists. That story, as it turned out, ended up being too lengthy for inclusion in this book and was produced in a separate volume, *Sacred Service in Civic Space* (2007). The present volume, *Called to Community*, completes the story as Dorothy had originally envisioned it, told in partnership with Anita Farber-Robertson, with contributions from Mary Ganz, Rebecca Parker, and myself. I am gratified that my account of the recent history of community ministry is included here with the experiential accounts of those who lived it.[1]

Central to this book is a conviction of the promise that community ministry offers—to the world as well as to our faith tradition—as it assumes a place of full viability alongside Unitarian Universalist parish ministry and religious education. These pages capture the story of the struggle and concern that lay behind the promise, as it was felt among those who understood on a deep level what it could mean. At one point or another, and for one reason or another, some feared the viability they hoped for would not be achieved. Despite the difficulties, however, Unitarian Universalist community ministry has become real—with both visionary and practical results—as

---

1 Please note that most of the manuscript of this book was completed in 2008 and reflects the ministries people were engaged in at the time. Some of these ministries have changed, and some ministers have retired or passed away.

is seen in the inspiring examples collected and shared in the fourth chapter. Finally, as the authors here note, the challenges that remain "can and will be met, and those who are called to community ministry will find support, nurture, and celebration within their Unitarian Universalist faith community" (Farber-Robertson, p. 7).

As I have stated elsewhere, community ministers "bring sacred service to civic space in the great profound hope that from our ministry in the common places of life will arise the gift of grace, for ourselves and for others."[2] For all who are called to community, and for those who would partner in support of their work, the record contained in this volume reminds us that the process of implementing change, while not always easy, is worth remembering for the sake of our common achievement and enduring purpose.

Kathleen R. Parker
Pittsburgh, Pennsylvania
December 13, 2012

---

2 Kathleen Parker, *Sacred Service in Civic Space: Three Hundred Years of Community Ministry in Unitarian Universalism* (Chicago: Meadville-Lombard Press, 2007), 11.

ACKNOWLEDGMENTS

This book has been ten years in the making. In 2003, the idea to publish a book on community ministry took root, and a proposal to fund it was submitted to the Fund for Unitarian Universalism. The proposal referenced an earlier manuscript developed by the Starr King Community Ministry Project in 1995, which contained the essay by Rebecca Parker that serves as Prologue for this book.[3] Two women who have since died deserve special recognition for inspiring this book: Mary Harrington, who provided inspiration and motivation for the Starr King project, and Jody Shipley, for her role in inspiring community ministers and forming three community ministry organizations: Society for the Larger Ministry, UU Center for Community Ministry, and the Community Ministry Focus Group of the UU Ministers' Association. By the time the three groups met together in Boston in July 2003, a grant had been awarded, and the book project was launched.

Over the years many people contributed to the development of this book. Dorothy Emerson conceived of the idea initially, wrote the funding proposals, and served as coordinating editor for the first two years. Jeanne Lloyd and Maddie Sifantus, co-presidents, agreed to have the Society for the Larger Ministry serve as fiscal agent for the grant. An Editorial Committee was established to guide the book process during the first five years. Roger Brewin, Barbara Davenport, Dorothy Emerson, Anita Farber-Robertson, Mary Ganz, Deborah Holder, Charles Howe, Kathleen Parker, and Maddie Sifantus all served for a time on that committee. David Hubner, Director of the UUA Department of Ministry at the time, was supportive throughout the process of developing the book. Others who helped along the way included Kendyl Gibbons, Dale Lantz, Margi McCue, and David

3 Additional details about the inception of this book can be found in *Called to Community Preview Edition*, ed. Dorothy May Emerson (Rainbow Solutions, 2004), 2–3.

Pettee. Without the hard work and cooperation of these people, this book would not have come to be.

Materials for the book were gathered together, and in June 2004 a one-hundred-page, spiral-bound Preview Edition was published through Rainbow Solutions. Contributors to the Preview Edition are Kate Bortner, Tom Chulak, Lucinda Duncan, Dorothy Emerson, Anita Farber-Robertson, Flo Gelo, Kendyl Gibbons, Ben Hall, Lara Hoke, Tom Korson, Steve Landale, Rebecca Parker, Parisa Parsa, Don Robinson, David Sammons, Sarah Voss, and Jeremy Taylor. A feedback page was included at the end of the Preview Edition, and based on that input, changes were made, resulting in the current structure of the book.

We were fortunate that a generous donation, combined with sales from the Preview Edition, and a second grant from the Fund for Unitarian Universalism, made it possible for us to continue developing this book. We submitted the resulting manuscript to Skinner House for publication and were advised that it needed significant revisions.

The Editorial Committee invited people to review the manuscript, including Roger Brewin, Tom Chulak, Barbara Davenport, Ian Evison, David Hubner, Tony Johnson, and Leslie Westbrook. Anita Farber-Robertson, a member of the Editorial Committee and contributor of the essay on theology, was asked to revise the manuscript to address the criticisms brought forward by Skinner House and other reviewers. She and Dorothy Emerson became co-editors of the book and continued the process of developing a revised manuscript. We offer our sincere thanks to all those who contributed to this book at every stage in the review process.

In the meantime, the General Assembly Planning Committee sponsored a panel discussion at GA 2006—"Community Ministry: Its Roots and Promise"—during which Dorothy Emerson, Anita Farber-Robertson, Mary Ganz, and Kathleen Parker made presentations based on their sections of the book. Kathleen Parker's history section was developed into a full book and published in 2007 by Meadville Lombard Press as *Sacred Service in Civic Space*.

The revised manuscript—co-edited and written by Dorothy Emerson and Anita-Farber Robertson, with additional materials by Mary Ganz, Kathleen Parker, and Rebecca Parker included—lay dormant for a time until the Unitarian Universalist Society for Community Ministries and the Unitarian Universalist History and Heritage Society agreed to publish it. With the addition of Kathleen Parker's Foreword and summaries before each section, the revised 2008 manuscript will now become available. We are grateful to these groups for publishing this work. We hope our reflections on the history, theology, stories, visions, and challenges of community ministry will raise awareness of the potential inherent in this movement to transform both Unitarian Universalism and the world around us.

Dorothy May Emerson
Medford, Massachusetts

Anita Farber-Robertson
Swampscott, Massachusetts

March 20, 2013

PROLOGUE

by the Rev. Dr. Rebecca Parker

This essay was first published in 1995 by the Starr King Community Ministry Project.[4]

How shall we not feel... "the heart-break in the heart of things"? A hand is laid upon us.

—*JAMES LUTHER ADAMS*[5]

One day when I was sitting quiet and feeling like a motherless child, which I was, it come to me: that feeling of being part of everything, not separate at all. I knew that if I cut a tree, my arm would bleed.

—*ALICE WALKER*[6]

Our orientation, our point of identity, is to powers that are creative and sustaining and transforming, not ultimately of our making but rather gifts. In a sense, these powers depend on us to respond. Our vocation is to point to these powers and to respond to them for the sake of freedom and mutuality.

—*JAMES LUTHER ADAMS*[7]

---

4 Rebecca Parker, "A Hand is Laid upon Us: The Theological Challenge of Community Ministry," in *Community Ministry: An Opportunity for Renewal and Change, a Report on Research and Reflection* (Starr King Community Ministry Project, February 1995) .

5 James Luther Adams, "Radical Laicism," in *The Prophethood of All Believers*, edited by Kim Beach (Boston: Beacon Press, 1986), 95.

6 Alice Walker, *The Color Purple* (New York: Pocket Books, 1982), 127.

7 James Luther Adams, 93.

These words of Alice Walker and James Luther Adams capture the central affirmations implicit in community ministry. If I cut a tree, my arm will bleed.

Community ministry springs from the recognition that we are intimately connected to one another and all of life. It matters significantly how we are with one another. We are capable of injuring one another by how we relate, or we are capable of affirming and assisting one another. Connectedness is a given of our existence. The only question is, what will we do with our connections? What quality of relationship do we desire? Love seeks responsibility and care.

The nineteenth-century forerunners of our contemporary movement for community ministry spoke of our dependence on one another when they articulated the claim laid upon us to deal responsibly and lovingly with one another in life. Joseph Tuckerman, founder of the Benevolent Fraternity in Boston,[8] a cooperative effort to minister to the needs of the poor in Boston's urban slums, wrote, "In every stage of his being here, from the first breath of infancy to the last of the extremist old age, everyone is scarcely less dependent upon his fellow beings, than he is upon the vital air and upon food."[9]

Tuckerman conceived of our responsibility to care for one another in concrete terms:

> Every individual who has the means...should feel his obligation to seek out and to know a few families with which he shall connect himself as a Christian friend...in times of sickness and sorrow to be their comforter; and in seasons of whatsoever to minister to their necessities.[10]

Nineteenth-century Universalists were also keen about a vision of human connectedness. Beginning with a theological affirmation of God's universal love, Universalism called its adherents to an all-embracing love for human beings. Thomas Whittemore, a

---

8 The Benevolent Fraternity is known today as Unitarian Universalist Urban Ministry.

9 Joseph Tuckerman, "Two Selections on the Christian's Social Responsibility," in *An American Reformation*, edited by Sydney E. Ahlstrom and Jonathan S. Carey (Middletown: Wesleyan University Press, 1985), 342.

10 Tuckerman, 349.

Universalist writing at the middle of the nineteenth century, speaks with fervor of this imperative:

> See, then, that there is a common bond—a tie—uniting the vast family of man. No circumstance of birth, or of color, no misfortune, no oppression; neither poverty, nor vice, nor disgrace, nor death, can sunder it.... Who, believing and realizing this, can be unkind? Who can be entirely engrossed in his own welfare? Who can be the oppressor of his brethren? Who can be deaf to the moan of the sufferer? To the plaintive entreaty of the poor?[11]

In the twentieth century, we have witnessed tragic denials of our dependence on one another and on the planet, and we are experiencing the consequences—in the holocaust of World War II; in the slashing and burning of rain forests; in contemporary American society's hostility toward the poor, we hear voices say, "I have no need of you. You have no claim on me." The consequences of this denial of our dependence include violence; a loss of a quality of life marked by civility and respect; increased insularity, suffering, and diminishment of our souls; and a planet at risk of environmental collapse.

At the same time, a deepened and renewed conception is emerging of the reality that we are bound together in one bundle of life. Process theology expounds on the relational, organic character of life, and denies that anything exists apart from relational interdependence with the whole of life. Systems theory, postmodern physics, and the biology of ecosystems all reinforce a relational vision. Feminist theology critically deconstructs the image of separate selfhood and emphasizes that we are "made from this earth."[12]

We recognize that commitment to right relationship is critically important for the survival of life. We know this is a religious issue, and we recognize that our circle of concern must extend to the interdependence of all life. We cannot focus religion in the realm of the personal and the private alone, or be concerned only with the sustaining of religious communities in which people minister to one

---

11 Thomas Whittemore, *The Plain Guide to Universalism* (Boston: Published by the author, 1840), 240.
12 Susan Griffin, *Woman and Nature* (New York: Harper and Row, 1987), 235.

another. We must give our attention to the public sphere, the whole of life. Our religious calling is grounded in life itself—life that calls out to be cherished and sustained in patterns of justice and love.

In these times "liberal faith has a peculiar responsibility, given its openness and belief in the interdependence of people," writes Clare Fischer.[13] "The church is a splendid site for the encouragement of religious citizenship—that is to say, an activism attached to a deep sense of religious faith."

Community ministry gives concrete expression to liberal religion's affirmation that the sphere of our concern is the world, as blessedly and inescapably interdependent and relational.

There is a second, core affirmation embodied in community ministry. It is the sense that we live and move and have our being in the presence of "powers that are creative and sustaining and transforming, not ultimately of our making but rather gifts."[14] This is the theological affirmation of liberal theism: the conviction that there is power present in life that creates, sustains, and transforms. Some call this power God, some speak of grace, or Spirit, or the deepest wisdom within us; some speak of "the ground of all relating," or of Love.

In affirming community ministry, we are not theologically neutral on the question of God. While we refuse to be dogmatic, doctrinal, or closed in our language, community ministry cannot fully be understood apart from the affirmation that there is something in life that "lays a claim upon us" and empowers us to fulfill that claim.

This claim has been expressed in the prophetic tradition of the Hebrew Scriptures:

The spirit of God is upon me,
because God has anointed me
to bring good news to the poor,
to bind up hearts that are broken,
to proclaim liberty to captives,
freedom to those in prison,
to comfort all those who mourn. (Isaiah 61)

---

13 Claire Fischer, Internal Document, Starr King School for the Ministry, c. 1985.
14 Adams, 93.

It was echoed by the Society for the Larger Ministry in its 1988 covenant "to respond to the cries of pain, to our own brokenness, and to awaken the healing spirit of hope; to...act upon the basic causes of human hurt and separation."

James Luther Adams speaks of the hand laid upon us as those creative, sustaining, and transforming powers present in all of life, within us and beyond us. This "love that will not let us go" urges us to claim abundant life for ourselves and for our neighbor, and leads us to a life of active attention to the places where love is most needed.

Affirmation of an ever-present spirit that calls, comforts, heals, inspires, and sustains is the basis for the priesthood and prophet-hood of all believers, and the foundation for the mission of the church.

If we affirm that holy power touches all of us, *is present in all of us*, then we promote an understanding that every human being has a religious vocation to live centered in that power, responsive to that power, and as a witness to that power. The gift of this power is free-dom—and healing. Its imperative is love.

INTRODUCTION

By the Rev. Dr. Anita Farber-Robertson

May we be reminded here of our highest aspirations, and inspired to bring our gifts of love and service to the altar of humanity.

May we know once again that we are not isolated beings but connected, in mystery and miracle, to the universe, to this community and to each other.[15]

—OPENING WORDS # 434, SINGING OUR LIVING TRADITION

This book is a testimony to the faithfulness of those who have answered the call to care for and cultivate our connections in mystery and miracle to the universe, to the community, and to each other; and it is an invitation to join and support them in that work. It has been a long time in coming—not because there was insufficient demand, but because the need was great and broad and seemingly too big to fill.

The essence of community ministry is captured in the stories of the people who perceived needs and invented sometimes wise and often imaginative responses. As we worked we were reminded of Howard Thurman's wisdom when he said, "Don't ask what the world needs. Ask what makes you come alive, and go do it. Because what the world needs is people who have come alive." Our community ministers have asked themselves that question, and done what makes them come alive. As you will see, they are very much alive in their ministries.

---

15 Anonymous, *Singing Our Living Tradition* (Boston: Beacon Press, 1993).

7

When pieced together, the fullness of community ministry is revealed. We could not include most of the stories, but we have captured a sampling in this book for your reflection and inspiration. Other rich stories and unfolding possibilities may be gathered in the future for another volume.

It is important to understand why we wrote this book, so that you understand the choices we made. In essence, this is an invitation to you to enter with us into the significant, even gripping struggle to bring community ministry in all its forms—lay and ordained—out of its infancy, through its creative development and into its maturity as a vital and dynamic part of our living faith tradition. The book has been written in five sections by different people, each with a distinct calling, expertise, and style. It seemed important to allow the contributors their own voices. After all, community ministry is an incredibly beautiful quilt patched together out of the diverse passions, places, and times of the people who minister. The differences do not detract, but rather remind us to look deeper to appreciate the textures, images, and colors that complicate and contribute to the whole.

Community ministry has a long and illustrious history within Unitarian Universalism. Attested to in a variety of places, it has been the activity of lay people filled with passion for their faith and compassion for those who share their world. It has been the activity of parish ministers who saw the misery and need in the streets around their meetinghouses and the pain in a world beset by turmoil and violence. For the good of their souls and their congregations, they spoke and they acted: for racial justice, for gender justice, for economic justice, and for peace. And they made a difference. But their work, while appreciated, was not always recognized as ministry, and had no place in the concepts we held of ordain-able ministry. We celebrate these men and women, the good they did, and the trails they blazed. They began the long walk that the primary subjects of this book—ordained community ministers—have taken up.

The story of ordained community ministry begins before there was such a category or designation. Its roots are ancient in our tradition, stretching back to biblical times. We have included, therefore, stories and history that convey the development of this important dimension of our liberal religious tradition in the names, faces, and movements that had no name for the work that they did or the calling they heard and answered. Mostly we tell of those who have been recognized and validated in their ministry through ordination, as they sought to find a place for their work in the world within an association of congregations. This is not to suggest that there were not others who worked by their side or in similar ministries without the mantle of ordination upon their shoulders. There were many. Their tales are rich, but that is for another book, for someone else to gather and chronicle.[16]

We begin this book with two essential documents. The first is the statement of *Principles and Purposes of the Unitarian Universalist Association*, our associational covenant, which provides the institutional and theological framework for the development of all Unitarian Universalist ministry. The second is the *Proclamation of the Society for the Larger Ministry*, issued in 1988, which claimed the authority of community ministry, identified its call, and created its first organization. This organization exists today under the name Unitarian Universalist Society for Community Ministries.

With the stage set by these defining documents and responding to Rebecca Parker's challenge to translate love into action in the world, we offer an examination of Unitarian Universalist community ministry in five sections.

The first, written by Dorothy Emerson, explores the question "What is community ministry?"

The second, written by Anita Farber-Robertson, develops a theology of community ministry that draws from the deep wells of ancient times as well as from the sources and experiences that have shaped and strengthened us in the present.

The third, written by Kathleen Parker, gives a few glimpses into the long practice of community ministry in Unitarian and Universalist traditions and then focuses on the process by which community ministry obtained formal standing within today's Unitarian Universalist ministry.

To deepen our understanding of the specifics of community ministry, the fourth section provides a narrative, "Community Ministries

---

16 See Kathleen Parker, *Sacred Service in Civic Space*, for some of these stories.

Made Real," wherein Mary Ganz offers a kaleidoscope of images and stories of people who are practicing lay and ordained community ministry today. So many wonderful ministries are being done, and our space allowed for only a handful to be described. We hope that this brief sampling will help the reader imagine an even greater wealth of possibilities than has yet been tried.

While the final section, "Visions and Challenges Ahead," written by Dorothy Emerson and Anita Farber-Robertson, articulates a host of challenges, please be assured that we believe they can and will be met, and that those who are called to community ministry will find support, nurture, and celebration within their Unitarian Universalist faith community.

May this book then help us "be reminded...of our highest aspirations, and inspired to bring our gifts of love and service to the altar of humanity."

I. WHAT IS COMMUNITY MINISTRY?

by Rev. Dr. Dorothy May Emerson

In this opening essay, Dorothy Emerson reminds us that community ministry serves as a vital form of ordained ministry alongside ministries in the parish and in religious education. As we become aware of the potential in community ministry for healing in the world, Rev. Emerson encourages all ministers and lay leaders to learn about and pursue community ministry to more fully realize that healing potential.

Community ministry is any ministry that seeks to bring healing and justice into the world beyond the individual congregation. Community ministry brings the resources of faith and religious practice into the secular arena to address brokenness, poverty, illness, and injustice of all sorts. As community minister Scot Giles states, "Community Ministers proclaim to the world by their visible presence that the church is engaged with the world...Community Ministry has the potential to be a whole new manifestation of religious service and may redefine, in the mind of the public, the purpose and value of religion."[17] Community ministries have been part of our movement since it began. These ministries that move outside the walls of churches to bring healing and justice to the wider community were officially recognized in 1991, when the Unitarian Universalist General

---

17 C. Scot Giles, "A Guide for Settlement and Training for Community Ministry," written at the request of the UUA Department of Ministry.

Assembly voted to create a third track of ministerial fellowship[18] called Community Ministry. The first track, Parish Ministry, has long roots in orthodox religion. The second track, Ministry of Religious Education, was officially created by the General Assembly in 1979. The establishment of three ministerial tracks demonstrated growing recognition that ministry takes different forms, moving beyond the traditional model of ministry centered in a single person who pastors a flock of people in a particular congregation.

Now that these diverse arenas of ministry have been acknowledged as important and vital within our religious movement, the process of recognizing and ordaining ministers is undergoing further transformation. In 2005, the UUA instituted a new process by which ministerial candidates are approved for ordination as Unitarian Universalist ministers, prepared to engage in any category of ministry. There is now one path to ministry, and if desired, there can be a specialization in parish, religious education, and/or community ministry.

No matter what the process of becoming an ordained minister entails, there are ministers who feel that their primary calling is to serve communities beyond the congregation. The community ministries that develop in response to this call create new forms of visibility and relevance for Unitarian Universalism in the public arena and enrich Unitarian Universalism by bringing our religious movement into connection with particular groups of people with specific needs and concerns—people who are part of the interdependent web of life of which we are a part. Through both ordained and lay community ministry, our vision turns increasingly outward, enabling us to seek new ways to engage our values and principles in the world and respond more fully to the call to put our faith into action. Because our movement finds its grounding as an "association of congregations," it is important to relate the outward vision of these community ministries to our congregations.[19] There are several ways by which this may happen.

Sometimes congregations as a whole may become engaged in community ministries, such as social justice advocacy programs or

18 Ministerial Fellowship is the institutional recognition of professional status with the Unitarian Universalist Association. Ordination is the induction into ministry, granted by a Unitarian Universalist congregation on behalf of all Unitarian Universalist congregations, calling a person to spiritual service in our movement.

19 The official name of the UUA is Unitarian Universalist Association of Congregations.

service projects to benefit people in need. Often lay volunteers and/or parish ministers coordinate these ministries, especially initially, but, as programs grow over time, paid staff may be needed to support volunteers and provide continuity and direction as the ministry grows. Unless the ministry develops organizationally, the program generally shrinks to accommodate the available energy or folds altogether. The congregation could decide to call a community minister to direct the specific program or to work with the congregation to develop additional community ministries. Working together, the congregation and community minister can expand and develop whole new arenas for Unitarian Universalism and in the process "proclaim to the world by their visible presence that the church is engaged with the world."[20]

More often, though, community ministries evolve out of the intersection between a particular minister's call and a community with which that minister is engaged. This is especially true today, in the formative stages of this movement. Community ministers generally develop their ministries in response to needs they perceive in the world, or they respond to those needs by taking chaplaincy positions in institutions such as hospitals, the military, or prisons. The Proclamation articulated in 1988 by the Society for the Larger Ministry expresses the deep commitment that calls community ministries into being:

> We, as people living in a world that is both dying and seeking to be reborn, who are shaken to our very roots by the massiveness and depth of planetary and human suffering, are empowered by a driving passion to bear witness to that suffering, participate in its transformation, and affirm the inherent glory of life.[21]

To launch a new ministry in response to a perceived need requires the community minister to have a strong sense of vision, a great deal of courage, and a clear commitment to stay the course until the ministry is established. In many cases, community ministers have to find their own financial support, sometimes working at alternative

---

20 Giles, "A Guide."

21 Proclamation of the Society for the Larger Ministry, Chicago, Illinois, November 1988. See the opening pages of this book for the full text.

occupations while developing their ministries. Where community ministries have flourished, often they have done so because of the ministers' entrepreneurial spirit or because congregations or other institutions have supported their work. Sometimes new community organizations have been established to ensure that the ministry continues over time. Whatever forms community ministry may take, accountability to some Unitarian Universalist entity is important.

Not all community ministers choose to be ordained. Sometimes members of congregations are inspired by their faith to develop lay ministries. After engaging in their particular ministry for a time, they may feel called to pursue training as a minister and seek ordination. Or they may continue to develop their ministry as a layperson and seek affirmation of their work as ministry by their congregation or other organization. In any case, what makes their work ministry is their sustained commitment to it and their recognition of the importance of bringing a religious perspective to their work. This may take the form of incorporating discussion of spiritual issues into the work, making use of prayer and ritual, and gaining acknowledgment from those involved that the work they do is for the purpose of healing and justice. Understanding social action as ministry moves that work beyond single campaigns for social change and places it in the context of the larger work of ministry and faith development.

Almost always, the ministries with which community ministers become connected become an important part of a congregation's identity and life. Sometimes community ministers bring the ministry they have created to a new congregation and invite them to incorporate it into their mission as a congregation. If the congregation embraces this community ministry, their impact on the larger community will expand, and the congregation will grow spiritually from their engagement with whatever larger community the ministry serves. Both the ministry and the congregation will be enriched by the connection.

Finally, it would be a mistake to assume that parish ministers are not involved in ministry to the wider community. In fact, as the Rev. Lindi Ramsden puts it, "Parish ministers better have a strong community component in their ministries, or else they're not living our faith. A church's ministry is about ministering—and that very quickly takes you outside the doors of the church."[22] As a practical matter, however, parish-based ministers may have their hands full dealing with demands for pastoral care, worship, and developing and supporting lay leadership. Unless congregations are clear about their mission to the wider community and provide support for their parish ministers to pursue this work, it often gets pushed aside by the immediate needs of the congregation. The presence of a community minister in a congregation can provide much-needed support to parish ministers, as well as to lay members, to facilitate "living our faith" in local communities and in the wider world.

The story of a community ministry's response to a particular need in a specific place has been replicated many times over, as you will read in this book. Unitarian Universalist community ministries are a visible presence in hospitals and hospices, counseling centers and schools, prisons, the military, police and fire departments, and in many social service and advocacy organizations and programs. Unitarian Universalist community ministers help people who are homeless find jobs and housing; they support women and children who have experienced violence and abuse in rebuilding their lives; they help congregations make their facilities more energy-efficient; they advocate for racial and economic justice, socially responsible and community investing, sex education and equal marriage, and the rights of indigenous peoples; they counsel people who are struggling with depression or dealing with life-threatening illnesses; they provide a context for college students to engage in faith development; they direct agencies that work for international human rights and seek to protect prisoners from abuse; they teach and serve as administrators in colleges, universities, and seminaries; they work for the Unitarian Universalist Association; and they work with individual congregations, clusters of congregations, and districts to institutionalize social justice ministries as a central aspect of Unitarian Universalism. All of this important work is accomplished by community ministers and would not happen—at least not in the depth and breadth that is now possible—without their being called to community.

ᔐ

---

22 Lindi Ramsden, interview with Mary Ganz, August 19, 2005.

With all these instances of community ministry being practiced, the fact remains that many Unitarian Universalists are still unclear about just what community ministry is and how it is linked to our UU congregations and our Association. Because of the often-idiosyncratic nature of some ministries, it can be difficult to understand the breadth and scope of community ministry or grasp its potential for the future of Unitarian Universalism. To foster an understanding of the whole of community ministry, it may be helpful to think in terms of different types, or categories, of community ministry.

The UUA Ministerial Fellowship Committee, the group responsible for evaluating prospective ministers, has defined five areas of ministerial competence in which they expect every minister to be prepared: pastoral work, prophetic outreach, teaching, practical arts, and worship. These areas of competency roughly parallel a more traditional model of "offices of ministry." Initially that model described three areas: priestly, pastoral, and prophetic. Later two additional forms were added: teaching or pedagogical,[23] and governance[24] or administrative.[25] Often these categories overlap, whether in community ministry or parish ministry. With community ministry, however, one of these categories more likely provides the central focus that calls the ministry into being. In a sermon, the Rev. William Haney describes the value, as well as the limits, of categorizing ministry:

> My classification into...offices of ministry is an orderly way of attempting an understanding of the mystery of the calling. Yet, each category is not an end in itself. Each is only a lens to assist in establishing roots, to find a grounding for what is and needs to be done in ministry. ...Often there are overlaps. Each category is not an isolated office, but part of the wholeness of ministry.[26]

---

23 William Haney, "Of Ministers and Ministries," sermon preached March 28, 2004, Unitarian Universalist Church, Columbus, Missouri.

24 Lynne M. Simcox, "Don't evaluate your pastor as an employee," *United Church News*, April 2001, www.ucc.org/usnews/apr01/pastor.htm.

25 Lisa Withrow, Church Leadership course description.

26 Haney, "Of Ministers and Ministries."

HEALING MINISTRIES (PASTORAL)

The largest number of current community ministers serves in pastoral or healing ministries. This is where the positions are in the outside world, and this is one of the major calls ministers feel drawing them to serve people outside of congregations. The pastoral role involves caring for individuals, bringing healing and empowerment to those in need, and making faith visible and practical in people's lives. Some ministers serve as chaplains in hospitals, hospices, prisons, military services, police and fire departments, social service agencies, and other public institutions. Others have developed private practices, including pastoral and other forms of counseling, psychotherapy, and holistic healing. These healing ministries touch many lives and bring Unitarian Universalism in direct contact with human suffering and need.

SOCIAL JUSTICE MINISTRIES (PROPHETIC)

Many community ministers and ministerial students feel called to serve in ministries that seek to bring justice to the earth and to people in our world who have been disenfranchised. They advocate for social and political change, working to empower both those with resources and those without to work together to create a more just and peaceful world. The prophetic role involves speaking truth to power, as the prophets of old did when they cried out against the inequities of their times. These ministries may include both advocacy and service, working with congregations and through community and faith-based organizations. In most of these ministries the focus is on dismantling oppression and instituting systemic change. Perhaps more than any others, these ministries provide a visible, public witness for our Unitarian Universalist principles in the world.

MINISTRIES OF EDUCATION (TEACHING)

Community ministries of education provide opportunities and empowerment to people in contexts other than congregations. These ministries may take shape in a wide variety of forms and contexts. Some examples include serving as campus ministers; teaching and developing curricula in seminaries, colleges, and high schools; leading workshops at retreat and conference centers; developing educational programs for community and faith-based organizations; writing and editing books and articles; providing life coaching; and creating Internet-based ministries that offer resources for spiritual reflection and personal growth. A primary goal of these ministries is to support and encourage people in seeking truth for themselves and applying what they learn to the way they live their lives. Through such ministries of education, Unitarian Universalist principles are made manifest and practical in the wider world.

Ministries of religious education within congregations are another expression of this form of ministry, and some community ministers may offer programs for congregational education in addition to their work in the wider community.

ORGANIZATIONAL LEADERSHIP (PRACTICAL ARTS)

Although many ministers feel unprepared to assume this role, the practical arts of administration involve skills that most parish and religious education ministers need. For community ministers, administration and organizational leadership often become essential components of their work. By developing this specialty, community ministers can help other ministers and institutions in this important arena. A number of ordained ministers serve in administrative positions with the Unitarian Universalist Association and in the various district offices. Others provide leadership in UU associate and affiliate organizations or community or faith-based organizations. Still others work as consultants with congregations and organizations, providing organizational development, skill-building, and fund-raising services. As our institutional structures develop in complexity and capacity, ministries of organizational leadership become more and more essential to our evolution as a religious movement.

MINISTRIES OF SPIRITUALITY AND THE ARTS (WORSHIP)

The priestly function of ministry helps people connect to spirit and celebrate sacred moments in their lives through worship and other ritual acts that affirm the central principles of faith. Community ministers incorporate this function as part of their work when they preach about their ministries in congregational worship or function as guest ministers speaking on a variety of topics. Others may provide music or dance for worship or rituals. Community ministers may also perform weddings, child dedications, and memorial services; some even specialize in providing these services for people who are not connected with congregations. Still others work at fostering people's connection with spirit through the visual arts, spiritual direction, or public rituals. This celebration of Unitarian Universalist principles, often within a secular or multi-faith setting, is a powerful witness for our faith in the public arena.

෩

Community ministry brings all of these ministerial functions to bear in community settings, in response to the needs and concerns of the world in which we live. Because community ministries can take many different shapes and forms, there are real opportunities for creativity and imagination to be employed, as we seek together to respond to "a world that is both dying and seeking to be reborn." Although we may often feel "shaken to our very roots by the massiveness and depth of planetary and human suffering," community ministry invites us to be "empowered by a driving passion to bear witness to that suffering, participate in its transformation, and affirm the inherent glory of life."[27]

Community ministry, both as a function of congregations and as separate enterprises connected to and supported by congregations, offers great hope for the world. There is no end to the impact Unitarian Universalism can have through the creation of community ministries. At the same time, community ministry can have a potentially transformative effect on Unitarian Universalism, by inviting all Unitarian Universalists to participate in an expanded vision of ministry. Further, it encourages us to respond to the call to ministry in our communities and in the world, as part of our spiritual development.

The words of a hymn frequently sung in The Service of the Living Tradition at General Assembly powerfully express the call to community ministry:

Wake, now, my vision of ministry clear,
Brighten my pathway with radiance here;
Mingle my calling with all who will share;
Work for a planet transformed by our care.[28]

---

27 Society for the Larger Ministry Proclamation, 1988.
28 "Wake, Now, My Senses," words by Thomas J. S. Mikelson, *Singing the Living Tradition*, #298.

II. FOR ALL THE SAINTS: TOWARD A THEOLOGY OF COMMUNITY MINISTRY

by the Rev. Dr. Anita Farber-Robertson

In her theology of community ministry, Anita Farber-Robertson emphasizes the bonds that connect us to one another, in this case to persons beyond the visible covenanted church-based community wherein no one is "outside the divine embrace." For such ministry, one must be "theologically multi-lingual," she states, and then demonstrates in numerous examples, from Clarence Skinner to Tom Chulak. Finally, says Farber-Robertson, the ancient priests and prophets of biblical tradition model for Unitarian Universalists the need for both inner and outer work—to extend our covenanted principles to those within and beyond our midst.

Every year Unitarian Universalists gather at General Assembly to conduct business, set goals, renew and create relationships, and to inspire and equip one another to do the work our faith demands. Mystically and magically through worship, memory, and hope, we reweave the ties that bind us one to the other.

One of the most moving of these times is the Service of the Living Tradition, when we welcome in those who have taken on the mantle of ordained professional ministry, honor those who are retiring from full-time service, and remember those who have died in the past year, leaving us their legacy of a living tradition. At such a time we often sing:

For all the saints
Who from their labors rest,
Who thee by faith before the world confessed,
Thy name most holy, be forever blest
Alleluia! Alleluia!

It is a song that evokes tears and love. We are remembering that we are standing on the shoulders of those who have gone before. And we are awed by the wonder of what they have left behind: a gift to be lived and a torch to be carried and passed along.

Who are our saints? They surprise us by their numbers. They surely are among the ordained and the not-ordained. They are those who have lived by the liberal faith we cherish and have made the world a better place for their having been here. Among these honored ministries are the ones who have brought the vision and the values of our cherished faith into the wider world, notably community ministers, people who engaged the forces of destruction, fought the good fight, and struggled with the powers that oppressed and denied the powerless. They have walked in places we were too timid to walk, and they have done their work in the name of Unitarian Universalism.

It is no wonder that we often weep when we sing:

And when the strife is fierce the conflict long,
Steals on the ear, the distant triumph song,
And hearts are brave again and arms are strong,
Alleluia! Alleluia!

We love them for who they were, for what they did, and for what they have allowed us to become. We love them for the models they have been and for the inspiration they have provided. We too hope to be strong arms and brave hearts. Whether we sing at the Service of the Living Tradition, or in our home congregations,

O blest communion of the saints divine!
We live in struggle, they in glory shine;

Yet all are one in thee, for all are thine,
Alleluia! Alleluia![29]

those words are infused with the spirit and power of thousands of voices joined, who declare ourselves the heirs of the tradition and participants in a community of faith, memory, and hope that transcends the bonds of time and holds us all in blessed communion.

THE BONDS MADE VISIBLE

The central task of the religious community is to unveil the bonds that bind each to all.[30]

With those words the Rev. Mark Morrison-Reed, parish minister and author, captures what is probably the most significant and most widely shared understanding of the religious life that Unitarian Universalists hold in common. He is making clear and obvious what has been the theological bedrock of the historic Unitarian Universalist faith—the belief that "we are not isolated beings, but connected, in mystery and miracle, to the universe, to this community, and to each other."[31] The connections span time and space, binding us not only to the future but also to generations past—to ancestors upon whose shoulders we stand and upon whose legacy we build.

We have insisted on carving out the rightful territory within those bonds for championing individual thought and promoting and protecting personal autonomy within that community. Still, the bond remains a theological presumption that has identified us throughout our history. We can trace it in nascent form back to the early days of the Puritans on this continent, when it was a sin not to go to church on Sunday. A person could be excommunicated for that sin. Excommunication meant isolation, not only from the church but also from the community. It was a fate near to a sentence of death—personal and spiritual, and maybe even material.

---

29 "For All the Saints," *Singing the Living Tradition*, hymn #103.

30 Mark Morrison-Reed, *Black Pioneers in a White Denomination* (Boston: Beacon Press, 1980).

31 Anonymous, *Singing Our Living Tradition*, #434.

Being excommunicated meant not being welcome in your neighbor's house. This story illustrates how it was in early Puritan times:

> In those days, in a small rural community in the New England hills, a certain pastor was confronted with this problem. A long-term member had not been to church for several Sundays, and it was the pastor's habit to go out and visit people on such occasions and talk about it. The pastor had a particular feeling about this visit, though. The man he was going to visit had served long in the church, and they had been through many struggles together. He knew too that the fellow didn't take most of the preaching very seriously. As his horse plodded through the snow, he tried to marshal his arguments.
>
> The man welcomed him with a terse "Parson" and ushered him into the parlor, where a crackling fire was burning. They both knew what the occasion for this visit was. They settled in, and in a few minutes the parson was carefully expounding church doctrine. Every now and then the old farmer would say, "Don't matter much to me." This went on for a while, and then they both lapsed into silence.
>
> In the silence they sat staring at the flames in the fireplace, nursing their cider. Then a bright red coal fell from the grate into the gray ashes. As they watched, the coal slowly lost its luster and took on the grey coloration of the ashes in which it was resting. The pastor reached out for the tongs, picked up the coal, and put it back among the flames on the grate. As they watched, it recaptured its glow and soon broke into flame. They sat for a bit of silence after that, and then the pastor took his leave.
>
> The old farmer never missed a Sunday in church again.[32]

It is from those roots that Unitarian Universalism grew. Our faith is lived and thrives in community. Contemporary Unitarian

32 Folk story, source unknown.

Universalism does not make the explicit demands on its members that our predecessors made. But for those who seriously engage the faith, there is an experience that generates implications for our actions and demands upon the heart. Morrison-Reed continues: "There is a connectedness, a relationship discovered amid the particulars of our own lives and the lives of others. Once felt, it inspires us to act for justice."[33]

We have a relationship with each other and with the forebears who challenged the religious assumptions of their day, those who championed new visions and forged new institutions on the North American shores. Although over time we absorbed some of the wisdom of the native peoples, it was the European, and essentially the English settlers who established the structures and understandings of what became congregationally based church life. We are their heirs, and although we have stowed much of what they bequeathed to us in boxes in the attic, their footsteps still echo in our hallowed halls.

The early New England church embraced the concept of the Visible Church (identified, covenanted saints) and the Invisible Church. Many historians are interested in the story and the principles of the covenanted Visible Church. That is understandable. It was the Visible Church and the saints who comprised it, wielding their influence and power, that shaped the foundation of our church structure. We less frequently examine the Invisible Church, although it was a dynamic part of colonial life. I propose that for our purposes, the Invisible Church is of greater interest; it is the body of souls in God's embrace who are not publicly included in the established covenant. In Puritan times, the Invisible Church was understood to be made up of those who were saved but who had not been recognized as saved, and therefore had not been admitted into the covenanted community of the faithful.

This body of Invisible Saints is important, as it is that body that determines the boundaries of the real and complete church and identifies the extent of the divine embrace. For those who are Universalists, the Invisible Church includes everyone. There is no one outside the divine embrace. Consequently, we find ourselves in a situation similar to the one encountered by our Puritan forebears.

---

33 Morrison-Reed, *Black Pioneers*.

The early pastors were required to serve not only the saints but also the larger community of sinners: the whole parish. In other words, everyone was their parishioner, for there was no way to know with any certainty the mind of God and the true identity of the saints.

We share with those forebears an understanding of a sacred responsibility for the entire community, which is our charge. But our current social patterns and structures of religious pluralism and the separation of church and state have created barriers with which they did not have to cope. Our tradition tells us we are responsible for the care of all. But the recipients are unaware of or uninterested in our perceived mission. This situation calls for a different kind of ministry from the ones conducted by our forebears. It requires a cadre of people who will work in the world with those who may or may not acknowledge their spiritual needs—those who need pastoral services but may not have the language or be comfortable in seeking it. It requires a cadre of people who are theologically multilingual and who can move in diverse theological contexts and provide support in both explicit and implicit theological frames. It often requires what I would call stealth ministry.

Parish ministers and ministers of religious education do the important work of caring for the Visible Saints, those who have bound themselves in covenant with one another in the form of religious community. Their roles can be traced back to the earliest Puritan practices on these shores. Up until 1650, it was the common practice of congregations to engage two ministers—one to teach and one to preach. Although these responsibilities are somewhat different, they were easily absorbed into the single role of parish minister. The focus of concern and accountability for the ministries of both preaching and teaching remained in the congregation itself. And so it has remained, to a large extent, since 1650. Yet the needs for ministry outside the confines of the congregation call insistently now, even as they did then. Consequently, in today's secular environment, it falls to community ministers to care for the Invisible Saints: those who are not, may never have been, and possibly never will be in a covenanted community but who, nevertheless, are God's beloved and need to be tended and companioned on their way.

The kind of care and companioning that serving the Invisible Saints requires spans a wide range of ministries and many different sets of skills and expertise. No one ministry can accomplish all that needs to be done. In the chapter delineating the various types of community ministry being practiced, Dorothy Emerson makes clear this important fact. We do know that among the community ministers already serving, there are people who are trained not only in pastoral care and chaplaincy but also who understand the issues and dynamics of effective community organizing. Many have developed an anti-racist/anti-oppression lens and know how to apply it. There are those who have a facility for being theologically multilingual, and those who are multiculturally competent. These are the skills that enable community ministers to function effectively and authentically in the non-UU and sometimes non-religious environments that are the context for their ministry. They develop credibility in the wider world, providing resources to congregations and often creating openings through which the explicitly religious Unitarian Universalist community can act and bond. Working with community ministers, congregations and their leaders, both lay and ordained, can provide effective restorative ministry to the world.

EVER CONGREGATIONAL, YET DEEPENING THE MEANING

Unitarian Universalism has come a long way since those early days of Puritanism, having jettisoned many of the beliefs and practices of that time. No longer does it define itself as solely Christian or even as theistic. Membership requirements have become minimal. Theological boundaries have been transformed, so that where once we were Christian, now forms of most of the world religions find some representation within the Unitarian Universalist community.

Clarence Skinner, who had been the Professor of Applied Christianity at Crane Theological School, was one who pushed the theological boundaries of Universalism, as he pushed the social structure of his community. Having established the Community Church of Boston, which became a center for prophetic witness and social change,[34] he was in the forefront of controversial events gripping the community, including the trial of Sacco and Vanzetti, two Italian anarchists accused of robbery in 1920.[35]

Over time, Skinner's theology became more open. A 1924 essay, "In Times of Disillusion," voices his bitterness but ends on a triumphant (Charles Howe suggests defiant) note: "The world has grown unutterably old...[but] I'll still proclaim the 'Vision Splendid'... God's unsurrendered! SO AM I!...I light the candle and—I DREAM."[36] Later works followed: *Liberalism Faces the Future* (1937), *Human Nature and the Nature of Evil* (1939), and *A Religion for Greatness* (1945). By the end of World War II, Skinner's religious position had evolved from an earlier conception of liberal Christianity to an all-encompassing, all-compassionate humanism. "Radical religion," Skinner now said, creates in humankind "a sense of the vital, meaningful relationship between [the self] and the universe." In this "radical religion," humankind would not need to name in any specific way the powers that exist beyond the self. Our "village stage of existence," he reasoned, required such "partialist" views. But our modern world requires a "cosmic religion" and demands that we "expand our spiritual powers" in order to "increase the range of our understanding and sympathy." To make this happen, Skinner believed, people must embrace "the universals" — that is, the absence of all barriers. This was the "essential human task. There is no middle way. It is greatness—universalism—or perish."[37]

Although Unitarianism and Universalism evolved to extend a wide universal embrace, the theological infrastructure that informs and shapes its institutional life was forged out of the Jewish-Christian experience and its theological premises. One of the most basic of those premises is illustrated by the New England story shared earlier. Specifically, that foundational premise is that human beings are best able to live and thrive in community.

---

34 See Kathleen Parker, *Sacred Service in Civic Space*, pp. 186–87, for more details about Skinner and the Community Church of Boston.

35 Michael Dukakis, when he was Governor of Massachusetts, issued an official apology to the descendants of Sacco and Vanzetti, the two men who were executed for the alleged crime, and exonerated them.

36 Clarence Skinner, "In Times of Disillusion," *The Essential Clarence Skinner*, Clarence Russell Skinner and Charles A. Howe, eds. (Boston: Skinner House, 2004), 17.

37 Skinner, 82.

At the Unitarian Universalist Ministers Association Convocation in 1995, George Kimmich Beach spoke about the covenant of spiritual freedom, turning to James Luther Adams, who said in *The Prophethood of All Believers*,

> I call that church free which in covenant with the divine community-forming powers brings the individual, even the unacceptable, into a caring, trusting fellowship that protects and nourishes integrity and spiritual freedom. Its goal is the prophethood and priesthood of all believers—the one for the liberty of prophesying, the other for the ministry of healing.

The Rev. Beach went on to explain that Adams's words echoed the famous lines by Rev. William Ellery Channing, minister of the Federal Street Church in Boston, on the theme "I call that mind free," from his Election Sermon of 1830. He noted, however, "Adams was making a significant shift by exploring the meaning of freedom for the church rather than for an individual person":

> Between the Channing and the Adams there is both continuity and a radical break: both speak of spiritual freedom, but with Adams, no longer the individual, but "the dedicated community" is the matrix, the birthplace of freedom. The dedicated community itself is the liberating reality.[38]

For Adams, covenanted communities do more than provide a specific place in a specific time in which an individual can make a religious home. They are essential carriers of the wisdom and the resources we need for our communities to do their work.

> Now, anything that exists effectively in history must have form.... Nothing significant in human history is achieved except through long standing communities. No philosophy

---

38 George Kimmich Beach, "The Covenant of Spiritual Freedom," in *The Transient and the Permanent in Liberal Religion*, ed. Dan O'Neal, Alice Blair Wesley, and James Ishmael Ford (Boston: Skinner House Books, 1995), 25–26.

of life, no religion, can remain viable unless it possesses a sense of depth, a sense of breadth, a sense of length (or continuity) in history.[39]

Here Adams is echoing the wisdom of Henry Whitney Bellows expressed more than a century before, when he said in his address to the alumni of the Harvard Divinity School in 1859, "Would that I could develop here...the doctrine of institutions, the only instruments, except literature and blood, by which the riches of the ages, the experience and wisdom of humanity, are handed down."[40]

William Jones, Unitarian Universalist minister and religion professor at Florida State University, has been engaged in research, training, and interventions to address issues of conflict and oppression. He has been particularly concerned with the systemic and structural sources and supports that make the pursuit of equality and peaceful coexistence so intractable. He too sees the power of institutions. "My thesis is this: In the postmodern world of oppression and expanding conflict, the preeminent permanent [dimension of Unitarian Universalism] that we must endorse and incarnate is the pluralism that marked our birth."[41]

Jones demonstrates that assimilationist models of social order invariably lead to conflict, as they require the dominance of one group or culture and the submission or oppression of others, establishing a norm of inequality. He notes that the integrationist model also seeks to eradicate difference, but through a process he calls blending.[42] Jones then offers a third model, pluralism, which he sees as having a significant grounding in UU history and tradition.

Pluralism, like integration, affirms the coequality of the "different." But unlike integration and assimilation, it eschews both definitive blending and cloning. Rather, "the

39 James Luther Adams, *On Being Human Religiously*, ed. Max Stackhouse (Boston: Unitarian Universalist Association, 1976), 17.

40 Henry Whitney Bellows, *Suspense of Faith*, 37.

41 William Jones, "The New Three R's," in *The Transient and the Permanent in Liberal Religion: Reflections from the UUMA Convocation on Ministry*, ed. Dan O'Neal, Alice Blair Wesley, and James Ishmael Ford (Boston: Skinner House Books, 1995), 163.

42 Jones, 174.

different" are retained as different, and this difference is regarded as valuable and indispensable for the new world order.[43]

Jones's insights about pluralism could help us as we consider expanding our concepts of ministry. As a parish minister and a community minister, Jones understands that institutions in general, and the church in particular, must make a choice to be either forces for change or forces to prevent change. He has hope for the potential carried in institutional Unitarian Universalism, because he perceives that the seeds of what we need to achieve peace with justice are infused in the essence of Unitarian Universalism. These are the seeds of pluralism—if we could only germinate those seeds and allow them to root and flourish. "If this philosophy of pluralism can inform our quest for the permanent, and if Unitarian Universalism can continue to incarnate this spirit, then the new world order can come."[44]

Bellows intended his 1859 statement to challenge the trend toward individualism, which was then developing under the influence of transcendentalism, and the commensurate devaluing of the covenanted historical church, an institution to which he was passionately committed. Adams and Jones also have perceived the need to champion the importance of the institutional body in the face of a perennial individualism that sometimes seems determined to destroy its host.

If the community is the saving/liberating body, as James Luther Adams, Henry Bellows, and William Jones, among others, would assert, who is responsible for extending that salvation/liberation to those outside the congregation? Is there a way to bring those "invisible" or potential saints under the umbrella, if not fully inside the covenantal tent that is the birthplace of freedom and the context for healing? It is into this role that Community Ministry steps—the role of connecting the unconnected and expanding the umbrella to provide safety and nurture to those not ready or able to take on the covenant but needful of its declaration of unconditional divine love.

The covenant is important—the explicit and intentional binding of ourselves, one to the other in community. However, the lack of a

---

43 Jones, 174–175.
44 Jones, 176.

covenant does not signify the lack of a bond. We are bound inescapably to one another, as Martin Luther King Jr. said, in a "network of mutuality, a single garment of destiny."[45] In the Buddhist tradition, James Ford tells us we find our inevitable bond acknowledged as the Jeweled Net of Indra.[46] In our own Unitarian Universalist principles, we express it as an acknowledgment that we are part of an interdependent web of all existence. However we express it, the reality is inescapable. The Great Community inhabits the "big tent" that enfolds humankind, in all its strangeness and its beauty. Community ministers, equipped to traverse the spaces between covenanted congregations, empowered and sustained by the explicit covenant they have embraced, embody the truth of the implicit assurance of divine acceptance and love, clothed in that single garment of destiny.

Through the adoption of Unitarian Universalist principles, member congregations affirm that meaningful faith and freedom develop within the context of relationship—with other people, with the flora and fauna with which we share the planet, as well as in a relationship with the force that animates, which some call God. The essence of healthy spirituality is a spirituality that is aware and intentional about maintaining right relations with those who share our habitat.

We see the centrality of relationship as a Unitarian Universalist principle in the writings and ministry of Joseph Tuckerman, who in the early nineteenth century began as a Parish Minister, but became a pioneer for Community Ministry. In studying Tuckerman, Michelle Walsh observes:

> Tuckerman's Christian theology is clearly rooted in experience, in a life of feeling and relation and natural interdependence, and is evangelical for the transformation of society and the world. In many ways his views are consistent with Channing's views that there is no original sin, though human beings are clearly capable of sin, and that there is the possibility of goodness and perfection. But Tuckerman's emphasis is on language that is more relational

45 Martin Luther King, Jr., "Letter from a Birmingham Jail," (April 16, 1963) in Juan Williams, *Eyes on the Prize: America's Civil Rights Years, 1954–1965* (Penguin, 1988), 187–188.
46 James Ishmael Ford, "The Lotus in the West," in *Transient and the Permanent in Liberal Religion: Reflections from the UUMA Convocation on Ministry*, 69.

and feeling, rooted in human nature where the natural impulse, untainted by social wounds, is to be empathic to the condition of one's fellow humans. This allows for the possibility of natural conversion to the woes of the world and an internal feeling of some personal accountability. [47]

This emphasis on the relational provided him with a "big-tent," inclusive, accepting religion, enabling and empowering Tuckerman to act and speak in ways that were authentic and believable to those who were disenfranchised, marginalized, and poor.

One way Unitarian Universalists embody this intentional relationship is through covenantal associations. The foundational covenant is the one that binds people together in congregations; these congregations then covenant together into larger associations, including the Unitarian Universalist Association, the Canadian Unitarian Council, and the International Council of Unitarian Universalists.

Relatedness, as a central defining theological principle, has been Unitarian Universalism's great strength. When the principle works, it provides support, encouragement to spiritual and personal growth, resources, and accountability. That relatedness, however, becomes a problem when it is exclusionary, overly values comfort and familiarity, or calcifies into routine and standardized practice, producing a church that functions out of habit and lacks mindfulness. The church is then poised to effectively shut out creativity and the call of the Spirit to engage in the world—a call that is its charge and the place that is its home.

The movement within Unitarian Universalist congregations to develop Small Group Ministries is in some ways an effort to address the needs for intimacy (relatedness) and ultimacy (deepest values and meaning) that members bring. Many ministers, both parish and community ministers,[48] have been developing and promoting these intentionally forged and supported small groups. They are relevant to our conversation here because experience has repeatedly shown that an essential element contributing to the success of such a small

---

47 Michelle Walsh, "Joseph Tuckerman's Theology of Community Ministry and Contemporary Unitarian Universalist Theological Struggles," unpublished paper, 2005.

48 The Rev. Calvin Dame, the Rev. Dr. Thandeka, and the Rev. Bob Hill have written about such small group ministries.

group ministry program within a church is each group's inclusion of a social justice/service project at least once in the year as part of its charge and covenant. The "relationality" that is being forged and deepened, therefore, is not only within the confines of the congregation but is also being extended outside of the walls and into the larger community.

The struggle to find a way for parish ministers and their faith communities to be led outside of their comfortable environments to engagement with a complex and often inhospitable world has been ours for quite some time. In 1986, well before the official recognition of community ministers who do the work out in the world and provide bridges for the congregations that seek them, Tom Chulak issued this stirring indictment and invitation:

> In the midst of a fragmented world, the people are coming to our churches and saying give me peace, give me comfort, give me love, give me hope... Help me to cope with my life. Let me know I belong. Offer me meaning and purpose. All of which people need. And the church is saying, "Come, I will help you. I will give you rest— rest that is so needed." Our churches respond, like so many other institutions, by dealing with the private, the individual. But who cares about the public life? Who cares about the whole community?

Chulak, then Director of the UUA's Department of Extension, understood that while the attention to immediate personal needs of congregants generated approval and affirmation by the membership, it did little to ensure the growth or even ongoing sustainability of the congregation. An interior, insular focus ultimately makes congregations ineffective and irrelevant.

> The privatization of the church, including Unitarian Universalism, has left it cut off from the public dimension for the most part. The church is picking up the pieces of private lives. It is dealing with symptoms rather than getting to root causes.

Chulak does not blame it all on the congregations. He identifies a deeper problem, one that is embedded in how we think institutionally about what is important. It is from those assessments that we determine what expertise our ministers will need to do their jobs.

So its ministers are trained in preaching, teaching and counseling, but not in sociology, economics and politics. In personal analysis, rather than social analysis. This separation of public from private has weakened the church as an institution. It has cut it off from its power. It has kept it from investing more significantly in community ministries.

We affirm in our UUA Principles that we are a part of an interdependent web of all existence. Yet somehow we often forget the context of our lives and our struggles, as though what happens to us or to our neighbors happens to us alone. Chulak challenges the micro vision that allows us to ignore our environment:

The public is the human environment in which the private exists. But as the public life has withered, the private life has become obsessive and anxious.

We as religious people need to emphasize communal well being, rather than possessive individualism, to emphasize the needs of the poor and powerless and marginal so that justice might be present for all. We need to empower the people to join one with another...in an expanding sense of responsibility for the community.[49]

The Unitarian Universalist ministry has rejoiced in nurturing the powerful positive attributes of relatedness in congregations. It was, after all, in that environment that those ministries were forged, validated, and blessed. The willingness to challenge the stultifying

---

49 Tom Chulak, "Community Focused Ministry and the Future of the UUA," keynote address delivered at the first conference of Community-Focus Ministers, Boston, November 13, 1986.

and stagnating aspects that emerge has been less enthusiastic and not uniform. Those who serve as parish ministers or ministers of religious education are embedded in the congregations and often are unable to perceive the damaging dimensions of practices that are familiar and accepted or to discern the creeping calcification that encroaches. The disruption of the congregation at whose pleasure they serve is unsettling, if not frightening, to many.[50] This often renders congregationally situated ministries tentative or ineffective in challenging congregational norms and practices that oppress or exclude within their own walls or in relation to the world beyond.[51] Rebecca Parker has said that Unitarian Universalists "hold to a core conviction that the realm of the religious always exceeds our efforts to contain it."[52] She is speaking here of the theological conviction that leads us to refuse religious creeds and doctrines. But while we may be somewhat successful in maintaining that theological humility and keeping our theological convictions permeable to incursions by the Spirit regarding our own individual, personal beliefs, our congregations have a much harder time of it. As institutions with history, traditions, and often endowments, congregations (no matter their theological bent) sometimes behave as though they have captured, if not contained, right religious wisdom, truth, and practice and hold those in sacred trust.

If it is true that congregations often do their best work when they are maintaining the well-being of the institution and its members, and if Rebecca Parker is correct that the realm of the religious always exceeds our efforts to contain it, we can see why there is a need for an extra-congregational function that is dynamic and institutionally validated but located outside of congregational life. That function can keep the "container" ajar and provide reminders of its deficits and its limits. It is this ecological niche that community ministers have identified as a critical arena for ministry to which they are well suited and in response to which they were called into being. Community ministers live and

---

50 This was documented through the research done with Unitarian Universalist Parish Ministers and Ministers of Religious Education, by the UUA's Racial and Cultural Diversity Task Force in the 1990's.

51 Just such a problem encountered by a Parish Minister has been the subject of conversation on the confidential Unitarian Universalist Ministers chat-line in July 2005.

52 Rebecca Parker, "A Hand Is Laid upon Us," 1995.

function as the bridge between secular and sacred spaces, becoming channels through which flow the dynamism of life lived in the boundary places, heralding societal and situational changes that seem to have an import for religious thought and practice, negotiating the impacts of change, discerning healing from hurtful movements, and shaping the development of public, private, and secular space.

Community ministers, using this understanding, are those who seek to engage the world grounded in faith but who function outside of the congregational environment. Some community ministers focus on particular populations within the secular community who have the need of love and service fueled by faith. These community ministers might be chaplains in hospitals or hospices, advocates in shelters for the homeless or survivors of domestic violence, community organizers of projects or organizations for social change, writers, teachers, or pastoral counselors, to name a few of the almost infinite venues in which our ministry has found a call.

In addition there are community ministers who understand their task as being the bridge between the covenanted congregation and the community at large. They work with, motivate, and equip the gathered community to open their gates, venturing out of their comfort zone and into unfamiliar places needful of their ministry. The Unitarian Universalist Urban Ministry (UUUM, formerly the Benevolent Fraternity) is an organization dedicated to that purpose. Its membership consists of Unitarian Universalist congregations who participate in the work of urban ministry through volunteering in their programs, sending delegates to the Annual Meeting, and financially supporting the work of the UUUM. When William Ellery Channing first set it up, he was himself a parish minister who saw the need and believed that Unitarians working in concert could accomplish more than any one person or congregation alone. The concept really took hold when at his urging Joseph Tuckerman took on the directorship of the program and became a model community minister.

ON THE SHOULDERS OF OUR ANCESTORS—
THE BIBLICAL TRADITION

The tradition from which comes much of our understanding of ourselves and of the divine is biblical. We have further enriched and thickened our grasp of the nature of those things that cannot be named or captured, such as the nature of humankind and the forces that animate us and our world, through other religious insights and practices from the East and from indigenous and earth-centered spirituality. But our common language and traditions are rooted in the Jewish-Christian scriptures, their spiritual wisdom, and the prophetic challenges they provide. It is this broad foundational understanding that has shaped us and to which we, for the most part, consider ourselves accountable.

From the time when God heard the cries of those who were oppressed and moved to release the Hebrews from the bondage of slavery, God created the congregation, the body of the faithful through which the saving actions would be accomplished and a relationship with the divine presence would be assured. God rendered instructions for the escape from slavery, for the solemn assemblies of rest and worship, and for joyous festivals commemorating liberation, all to be received and performed not as individuals but as members of the congregation (Exodus 12).

And over the years, when things went wrong, God looked not to individuals but to the community, the gathered congregation, for accountability and redress of grievances.

Thus says the Lord: Stand in the court of the Lord's house, and speak to all the cities of Judah that come to worship in the house of the Lord; speak to them all the words that I command you.... It may be that they will listen, all of them, and will turn from their evil way, that I may change my mind about the disaster that I intend to bring on them because of their evil doings. (Jeremiah 26:2–3)

Blow the trumpet in Zion; sanctify a fast; call a solemn assembly; gather the people. Sanctify the congregation; assemble the aged; gather the children, even infants at the breast. (Joel 2:15)

It is not surprising, therefore, that we understand that the divine speaks to a people, a gathered people, rather than to individuals. When God is represented as speaking to an individual, it is always as the designated messenger, the one who will convey to the people what is good or right or required of them. The divine relationship is with the people as a body. It is the task of the priests and prophets to keep the communication channels clear and the relationship in good order. The priests functioned inside of the temple walls, oversaw traditional religious ritual and practice, and instructed the people on what was required of them by the God who claimed them. This included the care of the vulnerable and those in need. *"Since there will never cease to be some in need on the earth, I therefore command you, 'Open your hand to the poor and the needy neighbor in your land'"* (Deuteronomy 15:11).

But there were also those who, while being a part of the congregation, functioned outside of it, offering feedback and acting as observers, correctors, encouragers, and issuers of dire warnings. We have called them the prophets, as their words were recorded and canonized—ministers without portfolio who surveyed the landscape and connected the community of the faithful to the world they inhabited. They span the biblical record from Joseph to Nathan, who lived in the royal court, and from Jeremiah to Jesus, who functioned outside the authority of courts, kings, temples, and priests. Always they answered to an authority they perceived as above or beyond the legitimated, temporal authority. James Luther Adams helps in understanding the position of the prophets:

The prophets were "political theologians" concerned with the destiny and the ethical significance of the state....

It is worthwhile to observe here...that the activity of the prophets was itself possible only because of a peculiar aspect of the social organization of the society in which they found themselves. The prophets could not have emerged had they not been able to appeal directly to the people. In this fact we may see implicit a principle of freedom that is indispensable for any Judeo-Christian theology of social action. The lines of political communication and activity were not held in monopoly by the monarchy.... Within the social stratification of their society, they were able to be the voice to and for the poor and the oppressed. In their tradition there was a separation between charismatic and tradition authority, which left the way open for prophetic criticism.[53]

Ministry then, in the biblical tradition, always happened in relationship with the gathered and covenanted community, the congregation, but it did not always happen within its walls or under its full jurisdiction. Neither has it always enjoyed the sanctions and blessings of that community—Jesus being a compelling example. Still, ministry as a called vocation, with its variety of persons, purpose, and function, finds its expression, rich and varied, in the biblical record. Often the people called are not the ones we might expect, and the ministry to which they are called can be as much a surprise to them as it is to the people they are called to serve. Yet again and again we are stunned by the efficacy of these ministries, carried on in venues neither they nor we would have anticipated, to do tasks for which they did not feel prepared.

God called Moses, who had a difficulty with speech, to become the leader of a people. Nathan, an unknown person, was called to speak truth to power. Amos, a shepherd, and Isaiah, a man of unclean lips, were called to prophesy about justice and repentance. Esther, a beautiful female orphan, was called to save God's people; and cowardly Jonah, to bring the challenging word to the people of Nineveh. God called Mary, a quiet young girl, to birth and raise a savior, and then to sustain and support him throughout his ministry. And God called John, a man wild from the wastelands, to announce the coming of the Prince of Peace. Each of these people was called to do God's work, and for each it was to be very different work. Were they not community ministers of sorts?

God called Jesus, a Jewish carpenter's son, to talk to fishermen, gentiles, and priests. It hardly seemed like affinity grouping or matching talents to tasks. The results were mixed. Some people listened, and followed.

53 James Luther Adams, *On Being Human Religiously: Selected Essays in Religion and Society*, ed. Max Stackhouse (Boston: Unitarian Universalist Association, 1976), 107.

Then God called people to spread the Gospel—Peter, who had denied Jesus; Thomas, who doubted him; Paul, a zealot who had never even met Jesus; and Mary Magdalene, a discredited woman to whom people would not listen.

Most significantly, since it is his story that shaped, inspired, and galvanized the liberal religious community, we look at Jesus, community minister par excellence and authoritative model. Yet Jesus is one who certainly would have troubled today's Unitarian Universalist religious authorities. He attended worship but did not participate regularly in any one congregation. He was an itinerant preacher without portfolio and without legitimate authority or accountability. He preached in congregations without having been invited and interfered with congregational life and practice by ministering to a variety of parishioners and contradicting the teachings of their local clergy. He was beloved by those who were poor and marginalized; he was a perpetual problem to the establishment.

Each of these people from the Jewish and Christian traditions did ministry, serving God and the people of God in their own way. No two of these ministries was the same. Not one of these people was ordained. All of them were in significant relationship with the community, as well as with their God. Were they the original community ministers?

This question can be answered only in hindsight, through the lens of history. First of all, we need to recognize that our question would have made no sense to them. We are looking to create categories to fit our world that were unnecessary in theirs. Secondly, it is only in the telling of the long story that we can identify specifically which dimensions of these people's lives and work ultimately mattered.

As we seek to determine whether we can properly call what these people did outside of the authorized religious context ministry, we can look at the outcome. *Beware of false prophets, who come to you in sheep's clothing but inwardly are ravenous as wolves. You will know them by their fruits* (Matthew.7: 15–16).

That criterion continues to serve us as sound and indispensable—judging a ministry by its fruits. It is the primary and single most important determinant of authentic ministry. However, sometimes it takes a generation before we fully understand the fruits of a

41

person's ministry. Looking back through the years, we have the assistance of elapsed time. When we are assessing contemporary ministry, we do not have the benefit of that vantage point. It is essential to retain the humility of a faith that understands not only that the realm of the religious always exceeds our efforts to contain it, but that it also exceeds our capacity to fully understand it. In the Apostle Paul's famous passage on love in his letter to the Corinthian church (I Corinthians, chapter 13), he reminds the parishioners that ideas, knowledge, power, and even faith are imperfect and incomplete, because we are mortal and only "see through a glass darkly." He summarizes this chapter on love by issuing one of his most memorable and challenging statements about the practice of faith: "Faith, hope, and love abide, these three; and the greatest of these is love." If the driver behind actions is love, the fruits will most likely be good. His is a call to compassionate ministry, tempered with a humility that will always allow for the possibility of admission of error and the consequent implementation of change. Paul's remarks are addressed to all the "saints"—to the people who populated the pews and not only the ordained, teaching, or preaching clergy. He was concerned about the ministries of the whole people of God and about equipping the people to do those ministries.

Examining the record of our biblical forebears, these people who ministered unauthorized by the religious establishment and to whom we look for guidance as we seek to cut a path through this new and unmapped territory, we are confronted with another question. While it is secondary to the first, it is important and illustrative nonetheless: How was their ministry validated—or was it?

This is very important, particularly since we are attempting to identify the elements that would justify validating, blessing, and ordaining community ministry. The answer is instructive. These ministries ultimately were validated and eventually even celebrated by the very community that was the target of their challenges and even of their anger. That the words and deeds of the prophets are included in the biblical record is a testimony of the people to those prophets' legitimate role and place in the story of God's people. When the canon was created, the community made a public witness acknowledging their calls. It said for all posterity that you cannot understand divine love and mercy; you cannot understand God's dreams and God's vision, without knowing that the divine is spoken on human lips, unclean lips, by people who often live on the margins of the gathered community. We need to remember that. And for all of our tendencies to question ancient authority and to criticize the established ways and institutions, it was their flexibility (albeit slow) and their commitment to serve what is holy that allowed and empowered them to embrace these challengers, acknowledging their place in the community, integrating them into the saving narrative, and bequeathing them to us.

WHAT DOES COMMUNITY MINISTRY LOOK LIKE?

Once upon a time, there was an island that had everything a people would need to survive and flourish. Its people had a rich culture and an abiding curiosity. This island was lacking in one thing. It had no fruit. People knew about fruit. They read about it in books, but they had never seen it.

A scholar on this island decided she would use her sabbatical to experience fruit. So she packed her bags and went by boat to the mainland. There she picked up her backpack, threw it over her shoulders, and began walking. She came to a local person standing alongside the road.

"Excuse me; can you tell me where I might find fruit?" The man directed her to follow the road up the hill and along some twists and turns. There she would find an apple orchard.

Our friend followed the stranger's advice. Each time she met passersby, they assured her she was on her way to the apple orchard.

Finally, following a turn in the road, she saw it. There it was in all its glory, surrounded by a neatly crafted stone wall. She walked through the gate. The trees were on either side, bright with white and pink blossoms. Our friend breathed the fragrant air deeply. It was beautiful. She wandered up and down the rows for a while, enjoying it all. Finally she was ready to taste the fruit. She reached up, plucked one of the beautiful, fragrant blossoms, and put it in her mouth. It was bitter. It did not taste anything like the beautiful aroma it had given off. Neither did it taste like any of the descriptions of fruit she'd heard so much about. Finding it unpleasant, she spit it out and took another, in case she had just gotten a poor example. The new one was just as bad-tasting as the first. Disappointed, she turned her back and headed home.

When she arrived at his village, everyone gathered around, eager to hear what she learned. "Fruit," she told them, "is beautiful. It has a wonderfully fragrant aroma. But its taste isn't very good—kind of bitter, and not really all it is cracked up to be."[54]

The moral of the story is, if you do not really know what you are looking for, you may not recognize it when you have found it.

So, what does community ministry look like? How can we identify it? Will we know it when we see it? When we do it? What is the essence of ministry, of which community ministry is one expression? Do the varieties of forms that community ministry takes share some theological principles? If so, what are those commonalities?

To answer these questions, we must return to our attempt to understand the complex vocation of ministry. If community ministry is to be one face of Unitarian Universalist ministry, we need to capture what the umbrella term of *ministry* identifies.

First of all, Unitarian Universalist ministry affirms and promotes the principles of the association. Faithful Unitarian Universalism recognizes and validates those ministries within its community that affirm and promote those covenanted principles in the world beyond the congregational walls. Truly, all Unitarian Universalists are called to affirm and promote the principles of the covenant. The call is issued for everyone, and the venue for which it is issued is everywhere. In the congregation, in the workplace, in the public area, and in intimate relationships, Unitarian Universalists are covenanted to affirm and promote these principles in word and in deed. All persons are

---

54 Michael Quinn Patton, adapted from *Qualitative Evaluation Methods* (Beverly Hills, CA: Sage Publications, 1980), 21.

called as ministers in some fashion. That is why, when James Luther Adams wrote about this faith, he accepted the biblically based reformation assertion of the priesthood of all believers and took it one step further, asserting the prophethood of all believers. The reformers who proclaimed the priesthood of all believers were claiming for the laity the full access to God in prayer, scripture, and devotional practice, without the need of a priest to intercede. They could offer one another healing, comfort, correction, and prayer. Adams proclaims the logical and implicit next step—the prophethood of all believers; the right and responsibility of all believers to discern what the implications are for public, private, societal, and interpersonal behaviors, and then be about the business of actualizing them. The prophethood of all believers means that each person must not only participate in public life but also critique and work to change it to the extent that it falls short of the biblically based and historically affirmed community of love and justice. We have heard it called the peaceable kingdom, the realm of God, and the beloved community. It has been described in books of the prophets and in poetic verse.

Then justice will dwell in the wilderness, and righteousness in the fruitful field. The effect of righteousness will be peace and the result of righteousness quietness and trust forever. My people will abide in peaceful habitation, in secure dwellings and quiet resting places. (Isaiah 32:16–18)

They shall beat their swords into plowshares and their spears into pruning hooks. Nation shall not lift up sword against nation, neither shall they learn war anymore. But they shall all sit under their own vines and fig trees, and no one shall make them afraid. (Micah 4:3)

My heart is moved by all I cannot save:
So much has been destroyed
I have to cast my lot with those who, age after age,
Perversely, with no extraordinary power, reconstitute the
world. (Adrienne Rich)

By whatever name we call it, and by whatever source we authenticate it, the claim that Unitarian Universalism makes on its practitioners is the responsibility of both the priesthood and the prophethood: of healing and repair, offering succor to the wounded and correction to the world that wounds. All of these are tasks of ministry. All of us are called to do them according to our gifts and capabilities. Some are called as laity, to bring this dimension to the places in which they live and work every day. Others are separated out for special training and special responsibility, invested by the faithful with trust and the power to heal and serve. Those people, we ordain. Some are ordained to the parish ministry, and some to the ministry of religious education. Those ministries are fairly well known and understood by our members, because the place where their practice of ministry takes place is primarily within the congregation. Those who come to worship, teach Sunday school, and work on the fund-raisers know who these ministers are and what they do. Community ministers, trained, ordained, and called to serve in the world, are more difficult to categorize. There is no set template of responsibility or function to which you can compare a specific community minister and say, "That is Unitarian Universalist ministry," or "No. It is not." There are some qualities, though, that define Unitarian Universalist ministry and give it shape, whatever form it takes.

Unitarian Universalist ministry, whatever form it takes, must affirm and promote the Association's covenanted principles. As listed in the front of this book, these are as follows:

The inherent worth and dignity of every person;
Justice, equity, and compassion in human relations;
Acceptance of one another and encouragement to spiritual growth in our congregations;
A free and responsible search for truth and meaning;
The right of conscience and the use of democratic process within our congregations and in society at large;
The goal of world community and peace, liberty, and justice for all;
Respect for the interdependent web of all existence of which we are a part.

These principles can be affirmed in a homeless shelter or a pastoral counseling center, in a consulting firm or prison, in a hospital or hospice. They can be promoted on the steps of government buildings, in a faith-based community-organizing project, in a job-training program for the unemployed, and in educational ministries to those who are undereducated. Doing a community-based ministry can mean attending town meetings or running for office, registering people to vote, leading antiracism trainings and workshops, or demonstrating on the Mall in Washington, DC. It means accepting one another and encouraging people in the free and responsible search for truth in a variety of places in this country or outside its borders. Community ministry can happen in an educational setting or a court of law—anywhere that people will be helped by encouragement to acceptance rather than disparagement and to searching rather than assuming what we know to be true. It means engaging in the democratic process and holding before us always the goal of world community with peace, justice, and liberty. Ministry—Unitarian Universalist ministry in general and community ministry in particular—will pay attention to the interdependent web of life of which we all are a part. It will understand the context of myriad relationships that are affected by what we do or leave undone.

All Unitarian Universalists, and ordained ministers in particular, are responsible for affirming and promoting these values. All of us have work to do—meaningful work, to which we have been called and to which, ultimately, we must answer. That work is our blessing, even as our tradition is a blessing. The work gives us purpose and fills our efforts with meaning. The tradition equips us to go out into the world—to places public and private, secular and sacred—and do that work with all kinds of people, accepting them as they are and enfolding them in the divine arms of love, even as we seek to release them from what holds them captive.

John Gilmore, Unitarian Universalist parish and community minister, recognizes the value of what we bring, and he advises us that, before we can successfully and effectively engage in the transformations we seek, we must understand and engage in the different levels of the work to which we have been called.[55] Using Matthew Fox's insightful analysis of the structure of the work, [56] Gilmore reminds us that we must participate in three different types of work: the *inner work*; the *outer work*; and the *greater work*.

> The *inner work* is the work of self-empowerment.... It is daring to get rid of easy, but dysfunctional, belief systems and take responsibility for our own actions and for our own education.
>
> When we do the inner work we shake off the anger, shake off maladaptive belief systems, shake off negative socialization, hatred and prejudice...until the real self, our true inner self, manifests itself right before our eyes. This is the inner work that we can do in (healthy) congregations... and is why strong congregations are so important.
>
> We also do the *outer work* out in the world, attempting to address the ills of society.

In his discussion of the third type of work, "the greater work"— the "work of the Universe," Gilmore reminds us of how this work is essential and integral to a responsible Unitarian Universalist faith.

> The greater work focuses on creating systemic change in the larger society, instead of working on the individual level.... It means going out into the larger community and working to transform it and the world and to make humanity's vision of a kinder, more just society into a reality. In our case it would mean working to bring about a world in line with our principles as Unitarian Universalists .... creating...the Beloved Community....
>
> As an institution—any institution, engages in the inner work, the outer work, and the greater work, it creates caring, healthy individuals in a caring nurturing atmosphere.[57]

---

55 John Gilmore, "Answering the Call to Community Ministry," essay submitted for publication in this book.

56 Matthew Fox, *The Reinvention of Work: A New Vision of Livelihood for Our Time* (Harper Collins, 1995).

57 Gilmore, "Answering the Call."

Ministers of religious education may do this work primarily with children and youth in our midst. Parish ministers generally do it primarily with congregations and their leaders. Ministry in the world at large that embodies and promotes these core values is a ministry that Unitarian Universalists need. Someone needs to do it, and someone needs to do it in our name. If we do not validate, equip, and anoint the people who feel called from within our ranks, this ministry will go undone, and we will have failed our calling.

Ordained professional ministry, I propose, is the activity that seeks to embody, teach, invite, and support the deepest religious enterprise. There are many compelling ways it can be expressed and embraced within the Unitarian Universalist tradition.

We have heard it from the prophet Micah, who asked what God required and received the answer: "*Do justice, love mercy, walk humbly with your God*" (Micah 6:8). Those words are the elegant expression of the UU principles in distilled form. The minister, as leader, teacher, healer, and servant, takes up Micah's answers, writes them upon the heart, and speaks them through the acts of ministry.

Jesus too, recognizing that most of us need complicated concepts captured in simple phrases (sound bites), offered this as the essence of faithful practice: "*You shall love the Lord your God...and...you shall love your neighbor as yourself*" (Matthew 22:37,39). Adding something to his instructions for his disciples, the prototype for today's ordained ministry, he specifically said to them to "*feed my sheep*" (John 21:17). Jesus explains, over and over again, both in his words and in his deeds, that the way to do ministry is to go where the need is great, and respond. Surely those in parish and religious education ministries can find an application of that charge within their venue. But it is most clearly a charge that is best carried out by those "free range" ministers who are out in the community in the places where the secular holds sway and the sacred is disguised. Community ministers, with their maneuverability, their varied training, and their ability to speak in tongues that are understood outside the Unitarian Universalist community, are positioned and equipped to respond.

Our own Ralph Waldo Emerson, an ordained minister who struggled to find his place and his voice within the Unitarian ministry, said this to the students graduating from Harvard Divinity School, "The true preacher can be known by this, that he deals out to the people his life, —life passed through the fire of thought."[58] Emerson, after trying valiantly and unsuccessfully to fulfill his calling by serving as a parish minister, eventually left the ministry to become a poet and traveling lecturer. He was still dealing out to people his life passed through the fire of thought. His tradition had no way of identifying or validating what he was doing as ministry. Sadly, therefore, tradition says he left the ministry. I suggest he never did. The professional ministry left him.

Henri Nouwen, a contemporary Roman Catholic theologian, wrote and spoke with a poetry, a conscience, and a passion that awakened and engaged his colleagues in the Protestant ministry. He said, "Ministry means the ongoing attempt to put one's own search for God with all the moments of pain, joy, despair and hope at the disposal of those who want to join the search, but do not know how."[59] His description of ministry is one of my personal favorites and, I believe, is adaptable, whether one is theistic or nontheistic, if one understands Nouwen's search for God as a search for meaning. However you might translate this understanding of ministry for your own theology, it proposes that ministry is not only about telling but also about doing. One's life becomes one's preaching, so to speak, as we who minister bravely walk what is sometimes a lonesome valley, because we hear the voice of love and justice calling.

Caroline Bartlett Crane was a Unitarian minister who surprised the world by inventing a community ministry through the creative perception of a need and the application of her talents. After serving as a parish minister for fifteen years, the Rev. Crane created a new ministry to neglected municipalities, developing a vocation of inspecting and improving public health systems and infrastructures of large communities. In today's parlance she would be called a consultant. Crane knew it was ministry.[60]

James Luther Adams, Unitarian Universalist minister, social ethicist, and theologian, spoke astonishingly plain and simple words when describing the work of a minister: "The vocation of the

58 Ralph Waldo Emerson, "Divinity School Address," in *Three Prophets of Religious Liberalism: Channing, Emerson, Parker*, ed. Conrad Wright (Boston: Unitarian Universalist Association, 1961), 103.

59 Henri Nouwen, *Creative Ministry* (New York: Doubleday, 1978).

60 Cynthia Gant Tucker, *Prophetic Sisterhood* (Boston: Beacon Press, 1990).

minister...[is] to form a network of fellowship that alone is reliable because it is responsive to a sustaining, commanding, judging and transforming power." [61] On first glance one might take this to suggest that the minister's work is confined to congregations. I think otherwise. What greater work is there for a minister than to be working out in the community with those who feel forlorn, forgotten, and afraid, and form with them a network of fellowship—one that could be their first authentic experience of reliability, because it is formed and validated, not by the values and things of the world but by values and accountability that transcend the current and often destructive authorities and powers?

While any of these definitions of ministry are valid, by themselves they are all somewhat incomplete. Woven together like a basket, they can together carry some of the variety and depth of ministry in general and of public ministry in particular.

In trying to communicate some of the essence of community ministry for distribution on a brochure, we coined the phrase "Outside the box...inside the world." I think that this is a conceptually useful way to construct community ministry.

EXPANDING OUR LIVING TRADITION

Community ministry always has "the box" in its story—"the box" being congregations, history, and institutional Unitarian Universalism. There are problems with the box, including conceptual constraints and common assumptions about ministry that can desensitize one to the ways in which the creative spirit is moving and calling. And there are strengths in the box that include tradition, wisdom, strength, and community, to which all ministry is properly related in some manner.

The people of Israel did not have our problem. The God of Exodus, the people, and the places they served moved as the people moved. The Torah was portable; it lived in a tent—a flexible, moveable box.

---

61 George K. Beach, *The Prophethood of All Believers* (Boston: Beacon Press, 1986).

From its beginnings, the American Unitarian tradition was strongly congregation-based, and although its founders began as emigrants, once planted in New England, they happily founded villages, established churches, and became townspeople. Unitarianism as a distinct sect or faith of its own, with its own polity, did not begin to develop until the 1830s. It was informed by the congregational Puritan roots it continued to claim as its own. This was evidenced by the Unitarians remaining in the buildings and retaining the name and the identity of "First Parish" in a significant proportion of Massachusetts towns. Those nineteenth-century Unitarians understood the tradition brought to these shores by the early Puritans as their tradition; and the Cambridge Platform of 1648 as articulating their theological beginnings. It is important to understand the significance of the Cambridge Platform. All decisions about polity, governmental structures, appropriate relations between authorities (including church and state, and minister and congregation) were considered in light of the Cambridge Platform. It articulated the dream, covenant, and mutual understandings that had informed and sustained their forebears. That Platform said, "There ought to be no ordination of a minister at large, namely such as should make him a pastor without a people."

The history of the American Unitarian Association was perpetually framed by this clear and unambiguous theological principle. Ministers needed "a people," traditionally understood as a congregation. "At large" ministers had no place in the congregational understandings of the founders. That was fine at the time when they had first formed themselves in England. But they were now in a different environment, one that begged for some new considerations. There were wilds out there, and a countryside occupied by peoples who were not papists, nor were they the identified enemy to right religion, the Church of England. They were indigenous people with their own religion and traditions. An alternative strategy needed to be developed. Our forebears were no longer dealing only with people already in gathered congregations, even if those congregations, by their Christian lights, be "wrong." There needed to be some way to launch ministers out into that territory, but there seemed to be no theological support for such an action. Therefore, those who chose to move out as pastors without a people, evangelizing the native peoples, created congregations as their first order of business. One such minister was Experience Mayhew, who evangelized and lived among the native people of Martha's Vineyard. Mayhew created a congregation of "Praying Indians," and in 1709 published the *Indian Massachusetts Psalter* for use with the congregation he was serving.[62] He was not understood as a minister at large, but rather as a minister with a people.

Occasional exceptions were made to the minister-at-large prohibition. In 1646 the General Court of Massachusetts appointed two ministers as missionaries to the native peoples, with the consent of their churches. It is noteworthy that it was deemed necessary for them to procure an action by the court to undertake such a theologically suspect enterprise.

This limited understanding of the role and place of ordained ministry continued to be true until the appearance of Joseph Tuckerman, who challenged and circumvented this narrow interpretation of ministry in the early part of the nineteenth century. His ministry began conventionally as a Unitarian parish minister in Chelsea, Massachusetts, and continued for twenty-five years. Yet he is often called the patron saint of Unitarian community ministry. Based in his parish, from which he could see innumerable social problems, he began the first "Society for the Religious and Moral Improvement of Seaman" in 1812. When he was forced to resign his post in Chelsea due to poor health, he was approached by his friend and fellow Unitarian William Ellery Channing, who was pastor to the Federal Street Church and founder of the Wednesday Evening Association, a ministry to the poor and unchurched in Boston's North Side. On behalf of the Association, Channing asked Tuckerman to consider serving as a missionary among the poor of Boston. Tuckerman accepted the challenge, and with the support and encouragement of Channing, his work resulted in the establishment of the Benevolent Fraternity of Unitarian Churches, which continues today as the Unitarian Universalist Urban Ministry with a membership of nearly sixty congregations.

---

62 Laura Arnold, "Indian Converts," Final Project, Reed College, 2001.

Later, when Unitarianism had established its own identity separate from the Trinitarian Congregationalists, and there was deep and troubling social turmoil, Unitarian ministers struggled to find their place in the public debate.

Theodore Parker, a Unitarian minister who became a voice for social justice that was wider than his parish, penned words we still use today in Unitarian Universalist worship. They suggest a part of Unitarian theology that offers a basis for supporting a ministry outside the walls of the meetinghouse:

> Be ours a religion which, like sunshine, goes everywhere;
> Its temple, all space; its shrine the good heart;
> Its creed, all truth; its ritual, works of love;
> Its profession of faith, divine living.[63]

Unitarianism's largely urban context also meant that it was confronted with some of the serious urban problems of the day. As the nineteenth century saw the cities' populations explode with the influx of poor immigrants and rural folks seeking jobs, there were those within the Unitarian ranks who responded—some laypeople and some in the ordained professional ministry. The most notable, because his efforts left us an effective institution that still serves the poor in the city of Boston, is the aforementioned Joseph Tuckerman. But his was an uphill struggle to create an appreciation and institutionalization of community ministry that would be accorded full respect and full compensation. In his report to his constituency in 1828, Tuckerman stated,

> The proposition...to allow six or eight hundred dollars a year as a salary of the minister-at-large has been met...with the sentiment that this is the work of an inferior order of clergy, and that the character and talents required for it are of a very subordinate class to those which are required of our pulpits. This, however, I think to be a great mistake.[64]

---

63 Theodore Parker, *Singing the Living Tradition*, #683.
64 Joseph Tuckerman, "Second Semiannual Report of the Second Year of His Service as Minister-at-Large" (Boston, Massachusetts, 1828).

The Universalist tradition was less bound by buildings and by place than was the urban-based Unitarian tradition. As a movement grown by traveling itinerant preachers who visited towns, villages, and outposts, Universalists were more concerned with invoking God's presence where they were, naming and celebrating it where they found it, than in creating permanent abodes in which God and the faithful could gather to connect. Dynamism, an essential feature of Universalism, continued into the twentieth century. In 1921, L. B. Fisher wrote, "Universalists are often asked to tell where they stand. The only true answer to give to this question is that we do not stand at all, we move."[65]

The yearning for enthusiasm and movement did not disappear within the Universalist heart when the Universalists merged with the Unitarians in 1961.

Gordon McKeeman, former President of Starr King School for the Ministry and one-time candidate for President of the UUA, articulated that enthusiasm in an interview with the Rev. Jody Shipley, one of the founders of the present Unitarian Universalist community ministry movement. As the Rev. McKeeman indicates, the enthusiastic outreach and connection that beats in the heart of Universalism, although subdued, clearly was not eradicated by its merger with the Unitarians.

> I think it's hard to work up the kind of passion and deep commitment that characterized Universalism when what you are saying is: "Well, we are UU's. We use reason. We believe in freedom and being tolerant." A lot of people believe in freedom and being tolerant. We're talking Universalist salvation here (slapping the desk). We're talking that every child of God is worthy, and that the point at which some one of those creatures is in pain, we are all in pain in the religious sense.... I think people want to know what they are supposed to be doing with their lives, for God's sake. Not just: "Well, we believe in freedom, reason and tolerance." You might as well go home and go to bed, for heaven sakes. I can be free, reasonable and tolerant in bed as well as I can out on the

---

65 [33] Ernest Cassara, *Universalism in America* (Boston: Beacon Press, 1971).

55

hustings [platform used for making speeches]. That isn't going to lure any money out of my pocket to do anything significant in the world.[66]

A key question before us then is: Do we do community ministry as an expression of our faith or as an extension of our faith? It is a question that triggers discomfort in many Unitarian Universalist circles. It has become standard practice for us to declare not only that we do not have UU missionaries, but also that we eschew them. McKeeman, grounded in Universalist theology and tradition, challenges that commonly accepted disdain for missionary movements and activities. He raises the worthwhile although disquieting question that must be raised in every generation: Do we have a message worth promoting and extending? If we do, what is it? If we don't, what are we doing here?

McKeeman suggests that we need to be doing both extension and expression ministries, but the passion for extension is the most efficacious for fueling them both. Although the task of speaking for and promoting our faith rightfully belongs to every Unitarian Universalist, McKeeman identifies community ministry as the role and vocation especially positioned and called to do that work.

It was the Universalists who were able to institutionally recognize the extra-congregational ministries of various sorts, because their understanding of God and ministry was not rooted only in congregational life, but also in the unconfined and often wild world outside. With a polity that allowed them to ordain by convention, they could recognize and validate those non-congregationally based ministries, ordaining and sending off people who felt a call to a wider mission. Herein resides the most significant challenge to our UU way of doing congregational polity and the most exciting opportunity for creativity. The challenge briefly stated is this: How do we validate and bless the extra-congregational ministries to which our people are being called?

Gordon McKeeman acknowledges the hurdle:

---

66 Gordon McKeeman, interview with Jody Shipley & tpkunesh, *critical* mass (invierno 1988).

At this point it would be a very difficult job to change the devotion that UU's have to congregational ordination. But I think it has some real limitations. Community ministries are often seen as dangling participles, without any connection to the main sentence. I don't think it is an insoluble problem though.[67]

The distinction McKeeman makes could be easily missed, and yet is critical. He is not suggesting a challenge or change to congregational polity. He is suggesting that we reconsider whether the congregation should be the only identified valid and viable ordaining body. In the Universalist Church of America, the state conventions (roughly analogous to our UUA districts) were empowered to ordain, and thus could and did validate, ordain, and send out ministers who were responding to calls to preach, to heal, to teach, and to comfort outside of congregational settings. We need that flexibility again. We need to be able to bless, empower, and validate those ministries out in the world that promote our UU values, that challenge the status quo, and that uncover and unmask racism and oppression where they are found. We need to do the holy work of *bringing good news to the oppressed, binding up the broken hearted, proclaiming liberty to the captives and release to the prisoners* (Isaiah 61:1). We need ministers who will help the divine hand in realizing the promise to *"deal with all your oppressors...save the lame and gather the outcast... and change their shame into praise"* (Zephaniah 3:19). We need a system, in addition to congregational ordination, for ordaining those who serve the Invisible Church and keep us faithful to our values and the call to implement them in the world.

Having built strong congregations and a strong parish-based ministry using the theology and polity of the Unitarian strand of the Unitarian Universalist tradition, it is useful to remember that within the Unitarian Universalist tradition is also the Universalist understanding of a mission in the world to which some are called as ministers, a ministry that does not stand but moves.

---

67 McKeeman, interview with Shipley, 1988.

A VITAL SPIRIT MOVING

This community ministry, being called into being by the passionate people who are doing it and by the world that desperately needs it, reflects the wisdom of the biblical and historic traditions and the creativity of a Spirit that refuses to be contained by any box we might construct. To the extent that we can weave open baskets to carry and support these ministries, the passions and the values of liberal religion will once again flourish, and we will be known as a people who not only have a stable place of nurture but who also have a vital spirit on the move in the world.

A warning: In wartime, the troops are most vulnerable when they have been advancing at a steady clip and have inadvertently outpaced their supply lines. Without supplies they cannot advance, they cannot do their job, and they cannot even survive. In the business world, when companies over-expand, creating branches, outlets, or franchises they cannot supply, they not only lose their investment, but also they may actually lose their market as their credibility is brought into question. There is an important lesson to be learned. While it is important to have Unitarian Universalist ministers present in the secular world, witnessing and working for peace and justice, dismantling racism and oppressive structures, creating bridges of cooperation and understanding, and healing and holding wounded people, they must not be out there alone. They must not be isolated, cut off from the supply lines of emotional, spiritual, and financial support. They must have a committed Unitarian Universalism behind them, ready to support and sustain them as necessary. We can find within our tradition a theology that supports and sustains Community Ministry. We can find within our tradition a practice of ministering in the secular world. The charge and the challenge to us is to find within ourselves an institutional will and a passion for that ministry sufficient to keep the supply lines open, equipped, and flowing, so that each Unitarian Universalist Community Minister stands in the world as a part of a team, no longer a lone ranger but a beacon and a channel for all the folks who want to join this religious enterprise and only need to be shown the way.

O blest communion of the saints divine!
We live in struggle, they in glory shine;
Yet all are one in thee, for all are thine.
Alleluia! Alleluia![68]

May it be so.

---

68 "For All the Saints," *Singing the Living Tradition* #103.

III. "LET IT RISE ON WINGS"— COMMUNITY MINISTRY ACHIEVES FORMAL STANDING

by Dr. Kathleen R. Parker

Kathleen Parker observes that community ministers in Unitarian Universalism have always been at the forefront of movements pressing for social change. In recent history, as cries for justice mounted in the 1960s and 1970s, UU ministers increasingly reconceived the task of ministry, which led such ministers to form new institutional groups, the Extra-Parochial Clergy in 1984 and Community Focused Ministers in 1986. This essay documents the emergence of these groups and their coming together to form the Society for the Larger Ministry (SLM) in 1987, which led to the vote in General Assembly in 1990 and 1991 to grant ordination to community ministers (alongside parish ministers and ministers of religious education). The Community Ministry Summit, convened in 2005, worked to resolve some divisions and setbacks that had arisen. At this time SLM took a new name—the Society for Community Ministries.

On a bright, crisp, Chicago weekend in November 1988, thirty-seven members of the recently formed Society for the Larger Ministry gathered at the Meadville Lombard Theological School. They were there to engage in a visioning process that would result in the writing of the *Society for the Larger Ministry Proclamation*. By Saturday evening they stood in candlelight, singing Carolyn McDade's "Spirit of Life," as each minister came forward to sign the document that had been crafted over the course of that day. In this shared, intimate moment of empowerment, they recognized together the necessity of their call to service in the world and claimed its legitimacy within the institutional body of Unitarian Universalist ministry. They were acting out of a long tradition, rooted in the soil of liberal theology and joined, in Richard Gilbert's words, with the "great living stream of reformers" seeking in all times "to create the Beloved Community on Earth."[69]

COMMUNITY MINISTRY'S UNIVERSALIST AND UNITARIAN ROOTS

Community ministry was practiced from the beginning of the Universalist movement in America.[70] John Murray, who became minister of the first Universalist congregation in Gloucester, Massachusetts, in 1774, also volunteered to serve as chaplain to the officers of the Rhode Island Brigade in the Revolutionary War. When other chaplains protested Murray's appointment, George Washington confirmed it with a commission. Thomas Whittemore was ordained into Universalist ministry in 1821 and served the First Universalist Society in Cambridge. Beyond the parish, Whittemore served as publisher and editor of the *Universalist Trumpet*. As a member of the Massachusetts legislature, he pushed through a bill to disestablish the Congregational and Unitarian churches of Massachusetts. Olympia Brown, whose ordination as a Universalist minister in 1863 made her the first well-known woman minister in the country, served for twenty-five years as a parish minister and then shifted her ministry to the wider community in her work for women's suffrage and peace. Adin Ballou was a Universalist

---

69 Richard S. Gilbert, *The Prophetic Imperative: Social Gospel in Theory and Practice* (Boston: Skinner House Books, 2000).

70 Portions of this essay are excerpted from Kathleen Parker, *Sacred Service in Civic Space* (2007), by permission of Meadville Lombard Press. For a fuller account of the history of community ministry, readers are encouraged to consult the larger work, a companion to the present volume.

parish minister whose belief in Christian nonresistance led him to establish a communitarian society at Hopedale, Massachusetts. Hopedale members comprised the most radical of reformers, living in accordance with Ballou's work, *Standard Practical Christianity*. Augusta Jane Chapin served churches all over the Midwest and in California. In addition to her parish work, she taught for a time at Lombard College, worked for woman suffrage, and led twelve literary study groups to Europe. In 1893, she was appointed chair of the Women's Committee of the World Parliament of Religions. Clarence Russell Skinner served for thirty-one years as Universalist minister to the Community Church of Boston, which he established in 1920. At the same time, he served as Professor of Applied Christianity at the Crane Theological School at Tufts College, and in time organized the Department of Applied Christianity. A defining feature of Skinner's church was its involvement in social causes.

Unitarians entered active community ministry in the nineteenth century, with Joseph Tuckerman's ministry to people living in poverty in Boston. He was appointed as minister-at-large by his close friend William Ellery Channing and the Wednesday Evening Association of the Federal Street Church. Tuckerman wrote, "It is the first object of the Ministry-at-Large never to be lost sight of...to extend its offices to the poor and to the poorest, to the low and to the lowest, to the most friendless and the most uncared for, the most miserable."[71] In 1830, Rev. Henry Ware Jr. accepted an appointment as professor of Pulpit Eloquence at Harvard after serving for thirteen years as minister to the Second Church of Boston. At Harvard, Ware served as inspirational professor and beloved mentor to aspiring ministers. When he retired early due to poor health, his students wrote to him, "Your example, beloved Sir, even more than your instruction, has taught us the greatness and beauty of a Christian life." Caroline Bartlett Crane, one of the leading Unitarian ministers in the Midwest in the late nineteenth century, began her community ministry while still serving as parish minister in Kalamazoo, by establishing the city's first kindergarten, a gymnasium for women, and an educational program for adults with domestic sciences, manual training, and academic

---

71 Charles H. Lyttle, *Freedom Moves West: A History of the Western Unitarian Conference, 1852–1952* (Boston: Beacon Press, 1952), 108.

courses. She later left parish ministry to work for improved sanitation and public health. Francis Greenwood Peabody, a Unitarian minister and professor at Harvard Divinity School, contributed significantly to the Social Gospel Movement through his teaching and his influential book, *Jesus Christ and the Social Question* (1900). In spite of racial discrimination in the AUA, Egbert Ethelred Brown established the first Unitarian society in Harlem as a forum for civic engagement among African Americans.

These few examples begin to show that the nature and shape of community ministry has reflected the changing conditions of human need across our society and within our institutions. From these examples it can also be seen that community ministries have often been in the forefront of movements pressing for change. The benevolent vision that imagines a more just and humane world has tended to challenge accepted boundaries in our social, cultural, and religious institutions.

In the decades following World War II, dramatic developments in American life brought into public consciousness the crises of racism, poverty, sexism, nuclear weaponry, and a divisive military intervention in Vietnam. The resulting Civil Rights, Women's Rights, Gay Rights, and Anti-War Movements, together with the War on Poverty, gave rise to a new sense of urgency for community ministry. Yet, as increasing numbers of community ministers emerged to address these challenges, they found that their work in communities outside churches could not be recognized as ministry by the Ministerial Fellowship Committee (MFC) because of the founding bylaws of the newly formed Unitarian Universalist Association (UUA). These ministers and their ultimate achievement of ecclesial recognition for their ministries will be the focus of the remainder of this essay.

COMMUNITY MINISTERS AND MODERN SOCIAL CHANGE

In the early 1960s, Neil Shadle and Ron Engel pioneered an urban ministry in Chicago. Shadle states, "Our awareness of urban issues was enlivened by the War on Poverty in combination with urban studies courses being offered at major colleges and universities." As a ministerial student, Shadle had been serving his third-year internship at a church in St. Paul, Minnesota. When the church experienced a fire, the congregation was invited to meet in the settlement house across the street. In these meetings at the settlement house, the congregation realized how isolated it had become from the community in which it was situated. When Shadle returned to Meadville Lombard Theological School, he designed his fourth-year course of study to emphasize urban ministry. After graduating, Shadle and his friend Ron Engel worked with the President of the school, Malcolm Sutherland, to design a program in urban ministry. Their courses revolved around such topics as social ethics, clinical pastoral education, and various kinds of chaplaincies.

For Shadle, urban ministry opened up a new way of doing theology, operating "in a mode of action and reflection." He states, "My work in community ministry led me to reflect on its deeper meaning. This led me to further action."[72] Shadle acknowledges, however, that, when they went to the New Ministers Conference in Boston in 1964, the denominational leadership discouraged what he and Ron were doing. "We were told that the UUA is interested in congregations and we had better be too." He concludes, "If I had not been connected to Meadville Lombard as a member of the faculty, I could not have been fellowshipped as a UU minister."

In this same period, James Reeb was working for safe housing with the American Friends Service Committee in Boston. He had left a position with All Souls Church in Washington, DC, which caused him to lose his Unitarian Universalist fellowship. Then, in 1965, he journeyed with hundreds of others to Selma to march for a voting rights bill. Tragically, Reeb lost his life in Selma when an angry white supremacist fatally crushed his head with a club. In our deep grief over his loss, few in the denomination publicly acknowledged the MFC rules that had deprived him of his status as a Unitarian Universalist minister.

---

72 Neil Shadle, interview with Kathleen Parker, August 19, 2004.

A first step toward legitimizing the work of such social action ministry was taken by the UUA in 1969 in creating a category of ministry called Specialized Minister. This category allowed the MFC to fellowship ministers whose ministry lay outside the parish. It led to the fellowshipping of Ric Masten, the troubadour minister from California whose poems and songs moved thousands to see his performances as ministry. Howard Matson's ministry with migrant farm workers was also approved for fellowship status, a ministry made "special" once he left full time parish ministry at the First Unitarian Church of San Francisco and made his migrant ministry full-time. Scotty (William L.) McLennan was approved for study to become a Specialized Minister. Unfortunately, the category of Specialized Minister was abruptly ended as "unworkable" in 1973, two years before McLennan graduated. Luckily, his status as an associate minister-at-large for the Dorchester area of the Benevolent Fraternity of Churches—Boston's long-time ministry to the poor, now known as UU Urban Ministry—gave him the congregational connection he needed to be fellowshipped. McLennan's later connection as a campus chaplain with Tufts, a school with historic Universalist ties, allowed him to keep his fellowship status.

Significantly, McLennan played an influential role as cochair of the Urban Church Coalition in the early 1980s in urging the MFC to broaden its definition of parish ministry. The Urban Church Coalition had grown out of the Center Cities Advisory Committee set up by the UUA. The Coalition was an advocacy group comprised of clergy and laypersons from fifty churches nationwide who successfully lobbied the MFC to open fellowship status in 1982 to ministers who were "pastoral counselors, chaplains, and community ministers working in prisons, universities, and hospitals—as well as urban missions and ecumenical centers."[73] This opening in the rules was an important development in that it recognized and responded to the changed tenor of the times.

The 1980s witnessed a proliferation of community ministers who were alive to the new challenges of the day. Orloff Miller was perhaps the first to engage in an AIDS ministry at a time when AIDS was little

---

73 Scotty McLennan, "A Vision of Community Ministry," in *The Challenge of Right Relationship: Community Ministry and Unitarian Universalism*, ed. Joan Gibb Engel (unpublished manuscript, 1995), 104.

understood, and people widely believed that physical contact of any kind would be contagious. James Zacharias, David Arksey, Barbara Holleroth, and Wilfred Ward established important counseling ministries, which were connected to area Unitarian Universalist congregations.

In the wake of painful divisions over the Vietnam War and the question of whether draft resisters should be granted sanctuary, Steve Shick accepted the offer of Eugene Pickett, then president of the UUA, to direct the newly formed Unitarian Universalist Peace Network (UUPN). Shick, who had been active in peace work through the 1970s, directed the UUPN until 1989. The UUPN was a coalition of UU organizations—the UUA, the Unitarian Universalist Service Committee, the International Association for Religious Freedom, the UU Women's Federation, the UU-United Nations Office, and the UU Peace Fellowship—brought together as a voice for peace and nuclear disarmament. The UUPN was the principle organization through which UUs participated in advocacy for peace, including our participation in the Great Peace March for Global Nuclear Disarmament in 1986.

Tom Chulak argues that a factor compelling movement toward community ministry was the Black Empowerment struggle of the late 1960s. The Empowerment Controversy, as it is sometimes called, left alienation and confusion in its wake when thirty out of thirty-seven African American delegates to the UUA's 1967 Emergency Conference on the Unitarian Universalist Response to the Black Rebellion walked out. They formed the Black Unitarian Universalist Caucus (BUUC), which created the Black Affairs Council (BAC) and took a separatist stance toward strategies for racial justice in the UUA and in society at large. Mark Morrison-Reed explains, "This black caucus tapped into the raw emotion hidden behind middle-class reasonableness. Civil rights had proved ineffectual at remedying black poverty, and liberal religion had failed to address the experience of blackness."[74] This painful struggle encouraged denominational efforts to search for ways to deal constructively with racial division. In 1983, MFC rules were changed to allow "dual UU fellowship" for African American ministers of other denominations. In

---

74 Mark Morrison-Reed, interview with Kathleen Parker, March 14, 2007.

1984 the Commission on Appraisal issued a report, *Empowerment: One Denomination's Quest for Racial Justice, 1967–1982*. Here was an important attempt to understand what happened and why.

The Empowerment Controversy generated significant urban activism, aimed at fostering leadership among citizen reform groups to challenge ineffective and/or discriminatory policies. An important model for this work was Saul David Alinsky, a leading Chicago-based reformer who organized the poor in the belief that widespread poverty left America open to the influence of demagogues. Then, in 1985, a revised UUA Statement of Principles and Purposes was issued, aimed at being more inclusive for African Americans and for women. African American minister Mark Morrison-Reed believes this new Statement was formative in offering a "transcendent narrative" that might help bridge tensions in the future.

Finally, community ministry in this period was sensitive to the gender revolutions of the previous two decades. In 1977, General Assembly delegates passed the Women and Religion Resolution, urging all Unitarian Universalists to examine the religious roots of sexism in the denomination and society. Under the direction of Leslie Westbrook, the newly appointed Women and Religion Committee convened representatives from the various districts at Grailville Conference Center in Loveland, Ohio to determine how best to address issues of sexism in the UUA and in the churches. From this work came a decision to revise the language of worship, which led to a new hymnbook, *Singing the Living Tradition*, and a new *Statement of Principles and Purposes*, in which language was changed to be inclusive and gender-neutral. The Unitarian Universalist Association approached Shirley Ranck to write a study guide that would help to implement the Resolution. This led to the publication in 1986 of *Cakes for the Queen of Heaven*, a widely used curriculum that explored women in roles of power and influence in ancient religions, through prehistoric time, Judaism, Christianity, and pagan belief.[75] It was followed in 1994 by Elizabeth Fisher's multicultural *Rise Up and Call Her Name*, published by the Unitarian Universalist Women's Federation.

---

75 A revised version of the curriculum has been published by UU Women and Religion: *Cakes for the Queen of Heaven: In Ancient Times* (2007) and *Cakes for the Queen of Heaven: On the Threshold* (2008).

During this time, the number of women going into ministry dramatically increased. Deborah Pope-Lance recognized this trend occurring after she had been ordained in 1978. Over time she served two parishes but in between developed a community ministry as a therapist to battered women in the Unitarian Universalist Counseling and Education Service at Belle Meade, New Jersey. Pope-Lance believes that the rise of community ministry cannot be separated from the flood of women entering ministry in the 1980s. From her counseling work, she could see that religious institutions were not well equipped to address women victims of abuse in compassionate and justice-seeking ways. She wrote a training manual for clergy and developed a community ministry as a consultant on sexual ethics in ministerial practice. Her ministry has addressed an issue made more visible—and more approachable—because of women's increased presence and consciousness in ministry.

Pope-Lance sees community ministry as a prod to the larger Unitarian Universalist movement to think more broadly about ministry. "My work," she states, "is challenging traditional expectations for ministry. It is ministry as activity and witness, where word becomes action and action becomes word." She describes the rapid emergence of community ministries in the 1980s as a response to social change. These developments provided the context for the formation in 1987 of the Society for the Larger Ministry.

FOUNDING THE SOCIETY FOR THE LARGER MINISTRY

Among community ministers there was a need to locate a community of peers with whom they would find support and affirmation. They felt isolated and invisible in a religious institution historically structured to recognize primarily parish-based ministers. In June 1981, thirty chaplains, pastoral counselors, and other ministers who worked outside of congregations came together while attending General Assembly in Philadelphia. They were responding to an informal invitation posted by Robert Rafford.

Rafford had been ordained in 1971 as a pastoral counselor in the United Church of Christ (UCC) and was fellowshipped in 1979 as a UU minister. In 1980, Rafford started his own UU congregation in Woodbury, Connecticut while continuing his full-time chaplaincy in Waterbury. What troubled Rafford was that he and others like him were not being recognized for their ministries outside the parish setting. It seemed to him that the single category of parish ministry in the UUA was closed and archaic, out of sync with the liberal UU theology he had come to embrace.[76]

The ministers who met with Rafford in 1981 were mostly chaplains and counselors, along with a few college professors. With a membership that reached forty to fifty, they continued to meet yearly at subsequent General Assemblies, and in 1984 they named themselves the Extra-Parochial Clergy. In the fall of 1986, they secured a grant to hold a pre-GA conference at Little Rock, Arkansas in June 1987.

In Berkeley, California, another group of ministers, seminary students, and lay ministers—all active in a wide variety of ministries—became conscious of themselves as community ministers. They worked in community service, peace groups, shelters for battered women or homeless persons, and a variety of social advocacy organizations. They found a mentor and organizer in Jody Shipley, who became ordained in 1979 after being inspired by her contacts with student ministers at Starr King School for Ministry. Shipley attended the 1986 meeting of the Extra-Parochial Clergy in Rochester as an interested observer. That same week, she also attended a meeting of the Commission on Appraisal and suggested that the Commission should be looking at community ministry.[77] At the conclusion of this meeting, Shipley was invited to attend a Convocation on Community Focused Ministries to be held the following November in Boston.[78]

---

76 Robert Rafford, interview with Kathleen Parker, June 21, 2005. The first vote to add religious education ministry barely passed.

77 The Commission invited Shipley to submit her concerns in writing, which she did the following August. Her cover letter to that paper, dated August 25, 1986, mentions having had "many conversations with students and fellowshipped ministers interested in Community Ministry." Shipley had the impression at the time that nothing came of her paper. No doubt her paper contributed to the long conversation that led the Commission on Appraisal to report in 1997 on "Interdependence: Renewing Congregational Polity," which addressed community ministry issues.

78 Elizabeth Ellis, interview with Dorothy Emerson, August 20, 2005.

The Convocation on Community Focused Ministries was initiated by Tom Chulak, director of Extension Ministry at the UUA, and organized in conjunction with the Benevolent Fraternity (later UU Urban Ministry). In November 1986 about thirty justice-oriented ministers and seminary students met at the UUA in Boston and in Roxbury. Both lay and ordained ministers were included. For four days they engaged in a visioning process to determine a course of action to promote community ministry. David Pohl, then Director of Ministry at the UUA, assured them that the Department of Ministry was "supportive of efforts to broaden our understanding of what constitutes ministry."[79] Ministerial Fellowship Committee rules had expanded the definition of parish ministry in the early 1980s, due in large part to the urging of the Urban Church Coalition. "These changes have broadened our definition of 'parish,'" said Pohl, "rather than establishing and validating 'specialized' ministries as such."[80] Here Pohl intimated that the expanded 1980s definition of *parish* established firmer institutional grounding for community ministry than had the short-lived 1970s experiment with the category of "specialized minister."

Pohl's address reported on the status of Unitarian Universalist ministry. Out of a total of 1,150 UU ministers, 640 were settled in parish ministries, and 100 were serving in ministries outside of congregations. (The others were retired or inactive.) He spoke expansively of the theological and ethical imperative "that calls us together in our search for a better world" and lifted up a shared vision of mission and direction. "Together we need to explore and support ways to reach beyond the local congregation, particularly to minister to the alone, the disinherited, the powerless, the battered, the shunned, the disillusioned, the overwhelmed, the alienated, the homeless, and the dying. We commend what you are doing, and what you hope to do, and what you would like the Association to do, to shape what James Luther Adams called 'the community of justice and love.'"[81] Steve Shick remembers how good it felt to be among so many like-minded

---

79 David Pohl, "Community Focused Ministries," address to the Convocation on Community Focus Ministries, November 10, 1986.
80 Pohl, "Community Focused Ministries."
81 Pohl, "Community Focused Ministries."

peers. "It was exhilarating," he said, "to connect with so many who were living out their call to community ministry."[82]

The community ministers at the Convocation adopted the name Community Focused Ministers (CFM) and formed a steering committee committed to the inclusion of ordained and lay ministers actively engaged in community ministry. The inclusion of lay ministers was one of the characteristics that made the CFM distinct from the Extra-Parochial Clergy (EPC) and would be a point of tension when the proposal was raised to merge the two groups into one.

The Steering Committee of the CFM held its first meeting in January 1987 in Boston.[83] Chaired by David Cole, then interim director of the Benevolent Fraternity, the Steering Committee applied for affiliate status with the UUA. This was an important step toward building institutional connections.[84] Coincidentally, the steering committee of the EPC was meeting at this same place and time for the purpose of planning their pre-GA conference. Not surprisingly, the close proximity of the EPC and CFM members at this site led to conversations about whether the two groups should join forces.

The EPC members, as Rafford soon discovered, were ambivalent about merging with the Community Focused Ministers. EPC reluctance was based on CFM acceptance of lay ministers. "We were trying to get a conservative institution to recognize our status outside the parish," stated Rafford. "The idea that we would include lay ministers seemed too radical and might jeopardize our standing in the UUA even more."[85] As for the CFM, they worried that the EPC were too conservative and lacking in innovative spirit.

Discussions among the EPC and CFM evolved toward a shared sense of alignment. In spite of their differences, there were already instances of overlapping membership. Moreover, they had a mutual purpose in their "concern for the further involvement of community ministry in the life of our UU movement."[86] When they came together

---

82 Stephen Shick, interview with Kathleen Parker, March 26, 2005.

83 Beside Cole, the Steering Committee included Jody Shipley, Susan Starr, Jane Boyajian, Stephen Shick, John Frazier, and Thom Payne.

84 The UUA Board later voted on and approved the affiliate status of CFM.

85 Robert Rafford, interview with Kathleen Parker, September 24, 2005.

86 This statement is quoted from a Bay Area Ministries Brochure, representing the co-ministry of Jody Shipley and her partner, Marilyn Gentile, ACSW, a counselor to the Gay and Lesbian Program at the

at General Assembly in Little Rock, Arkansas in 1987, leaders from both groups worked long hours to draft bylaws for the combined group. They agreed to a name—the Society for the Larger Ministry (SLM)—because it would neither exclude nor privilege either constituent group or any potential members, whether they were ordained or lay ministers. The formation of SLM marked a watershed moment of shared vision and common ministry, which enabled a consolidated movement to advocate on behalf of its purposes.

The first official meeting of the Society for the Larger Ministry took place in Berkeley in November 1987.[87] Thirty-five area UU leaders joined the fifty-four conference participants and, as Jody Shipley reported, "community ministers stood and introduced themselves and received a warm welcome and recognition." She added, "For the many UUs who envision a wider ministry in our movement, this was a very special moment."[88] At the next General Assembly, in June 1988, the UUA's Department of Social Justice presented the Holmes-Weatherly Award to the SLM. This is the most important social justice award given out at GA. Shipley took it as an opportunity to remind SLM members that this remarkable show of support recognized the value of their individual ministries.[89] Many community ministers appreciated this type of mentoring from Shipley. She was vital to their sense of empowerment in ministry; her community ministry was centered in nurturing their ministries.

The next SLM conference met in November 1988 at Meadville Lombard Theological School in Chicago and took as its theme "Continuing the Conversation." It was an appropriate title because everyone felt, with much optimism, that they were picking up the conversation where they had left off the year before. Spencer Lavan, president of Meadville Lombard from 1988 to 1996, recalls that there was a lot of questioning going on, as people earnestly sought to assess the importance and relevance of their work in the context of their

---

University of California at Berkeley Counseling Center. Gentile also served on the UUA Women and Religion Committee, ran a private therapy practice, and taught Pastoral Counseling at Starr King School for the Ministry.

87 Members of the Planning Committee included David Gilmartin, Til Evans, Marilyn Gentile, Susan Starr, and Jody Shipley, chair.

88 Report on the Conference of the Society for the Larger Ministry, November 6–8, 1987, Berkeley, California.

89 The Holmes-Weatherly Award is one of the major awards given out at GA.

UU faith and its institutions.[90] Thanks to a grant from the UU Grants Panel, a facilitator was engaged to help guide the conversation.

A significant topic of conversation was whether the membership of SLM should include lay ministers. After significant debate, carried over from the Berkeley meeting in 1987, the decision overwhelmingly came down on the side of inclusiveness. The Society for the Larger Ministry would be open to laypersons as well as clergy "who are in harmony with the purposes of the Society."[91] As Jody Shipley wrote, "The simple measure of good practice is in the question, 'Is what I do empowering to those I serve?' It is a question that tests all action... that separates out ministry that is self-serving from real ministry."[92] Attendees at the Chicago conference met in ministry working groups focused on pastoral counseling, chaplaincy, peace and justice ministries, community/urban ministries, academic ministries, and healing ministries. The groups formulated position papers that were carefully integrated into what became known as the *Society for the Larger Ministry Proclamation*.[93] The importance of the *Proclamation* was that it united the widely varying community ministers behind a common identity and mission, defined in broadly inclusive terms.

The opening lines read, "We, as people living in a world that is both dying and seeking to be reborn, who are shaken to our very roots by the massiveness and depth of planetary suffering, are empowered by a driving passion to bear witness to that suffering, participate in its transformation, and affirm the inherent glory of life." Neil Gerdes, librarian at Meadville Lombard, reflected that "the synthesis produced [in this process] resulted from ideas collected over the previous year. People were elated when it was over. There was a great feeling of euphoria and solidarity."[94]

That evening, SLM members came forward one by one, as they were inwardly moved, to sign the Proclamation. Judy Morris remembers, "We signed that statement finally in candle light, and I sang harmony with Carolyn McDade on 'Spirit of Life,' the hymn Carolyn

---

90 Spencer Lavan, interview with Kathleen Parker, August 6, 2004.

91 Bylaws of the Society for the Larger Ministry, 1994.

92 Jody Shipley, "Reflection on the Theological Sustenance for Good Practice in Community Ministry," unpublished paper, 1987.

93 The full text of the Proclamation is found in the front matter of this book.

94 Neil Gerdes, interview with Kathleen Parker, August 3, 2004.

had written."[95] The *Proclamation* described SLM as "a Unitarian Universalist movement of lay ministers and ordained clergy committed to promoting a broad spectrum of healing and social justice ministries." It declared, "We believe that only through many diverse forms of ministry can we heal the broken, create justice, and live in harmony with the spirit of life. We hold a vision of a larger ministry that sees the world as its parish."[96]

The next morning, November 13, 1988, several of these same ministers held a worship service across the street at the First Unitarian Church of Chicago. David Arksey, Jody Shipley, and Carolyn McDade jointly delivered the sermon, "Community Ministry in Our Midst: A Voice for Justice." Arksey, the minister-at-large at the First Church, spoke of the numerous community ministries historically supported by the Chicago church. These ministries, he stated, "have continued to actively make manifest this church's belief in a ministry of justice and hope for those who are most in need."[97] Shipley added, "During this weekend we talked about ministry. We shared visions of ministry that reach with our imaginations into the world we are all called to serve. There is a spirit moving through us. By 'us' I mean Unitarian Universalists. It is deep and it is hungry. [The spirit] is calling us to declare our mission...and without reservation to carry that mission out."[98]

After this, activity moved toward building connections between SLM and UUA structures of ministry, and seeing community ministry as professional ministry. SLM formed a Task Force on Ministerial Fellowship, chaired by Steve Shick, to promote a positive relationship between SLM and the Unitarian Universalist Ministers Association and to engage in dialogue with the Ministerial Fellowship Committee

95 Carolyn McDade, "Spirit of Life," *Singing the Living Tradition* (Boston: Beacon Press, 1993), #123.

96 The original signers of the Proclamation were Robert Rafford, Neil Gerdes, Orloff Miller, Melvin Hoover, James Zacharias, David Dalrimple, Roberta King Mitchell, Elinor Berke, Susi Pangerl, Linda Hart, Karuna Alan Kistler, Shermie Schafer, Judy Morris, Jody Shipley, Carolyn McDade, Karla Hansen, Cheng Imm Tan, Joseph Chancey, Richard Rodes, Lila Forest, Douglas Strong, Catherine Cogan, Thomas Payne, Stephen Shick, Spencer Lavan, Lillie McGauran, Neil Shadle, John Weston, Stephanie Nichols, Thomas Chulak, John Godbey, Carolyn Mitchell, Susan Grubb, Florence Gelo, Thomas Wakely, Ben Tousley, and Penny Hackett-Evans.

97 David Arksey, unpublished notes for a sermon given at First Unitarian Church, Chicago, Illinois, November 13, 1988.

98 Jody Shipley, unpublished notes for a sermon given at First Unitarian Church, Chicago, Illinois, November 1988.

and the UUA Department of Ministry. When the Commission on Appraisal (COA) began a study of ministry, it was reminded to consider the concerns of community ministers. Charles Howe, a representative of the COA, urged the UUA Board at its 1989 meeting to pay more attention to community ministry. "There is a tidal wave fast approaching, made up of many people eager to do community ministry," he warned, "and the UUA needs to get ready for it before it hits."[99]

After many months of dialogue, the Ministerial Fellowship Committee recommended adding community ministry as a recognized option for UU ministry.[100] In 1990 the General Assembly held the first of two annual votes required to make the change, proposing to reword the bylaws to add community ministry as one of three tracks of ministry that already included tracks for parish and religious education ministries. In May 1991, one month before the final vote at GA, the UUA's Task Force on Community Ministry was quoted as saying, "We urge settled Parish Ministers and Ministers of Religious Education to make themselves aware of community ministries in their areas and to encourage them and to embrace them to the fullest extent possible."[101]

The much-anticipated vote took place at the 1991 General Assembly in Hollywood, Florida. Prior to the vote, David Pohl, Director of the Department of Ministry, spoke directly about the proposed bylaw amendment: "An affirmative vote...will enable us to formally validate this ministry, adopt appropriate academic and professional requirements for its various forms, and broaden our understanding of how and where we may place our particular gifts at the service of our free faith." The General Assembly unanimously passed the bylaw change establishing community ministry as a third track of UU ministry, with no delegates speaking against it.[102] SLM

---

99 Charles Howe, interview with Kathleen Parker, September 1, 2005. The Commission on Appraisal released its report in 1992. Titled "Our Professional Ministry," it gave significant attention to community ministry.

100 The text of the bylaws change and the rationale for it was printed in the May 1990 issue of *Crossroads*, SLM's newsletter.

101 *Crossroads*, May 1991.

102 The amended bylaw (Article XI, Section C-11.1) reads in part: "Fellowship may be for the purposes of parish, religious education, and/or community ministry as determined by action of the Ministerial Fellowship Committee."

members were elated. Pohl articulated warm support for the change. "Your choice [of community ministry] makes you neither nobler nor less than your colleagues in the parish. To paraphrase Paul: 'There are varieties of gifts, but the same ministry. There are varieties of service, but the same ministry.'"[103] Community ministers agreed and looked forward to the future with optimism. They fully recognized the momentousness of what had just taken place.

COMMUNITY MINISTRY AS AN OFFICIAL TRACK OF UU MINISTRY

Soon after the 1991 vote, questions surfaced as to how community ministries might be carried out. To settle these questions, Steve Shick and Cheng Imm Tan were appointed by the Society for the Larger Ministry to the Liaison Committee working with the UUA and the Ministerial Fellowship Committee. The MFC assigned a subcommittee to work on appropriate academic requirements for community ministry candidates, internship sites, and renewal terms for community ministers in preliminary fellowship.[104] The SLM Steering Committee drafted a proposal to the MFC for the grand-parenting in of existing community ministers. Plans were also drawn up to confer with established community ministers to identify possible mentors for new community ministers in preliminary fellowship. Finally, SLM requested that a community minister serve on the Ministerial Fellowship Committee. This was made possible with an amendment to the UUA bylaws in 1993, and Ralph Mero became the first community minister on the MFC.[105]

Many became fellowshipped for community ministry they were already doing. Neil Gerdes had previously been fellowshipped as a parish minister because of his position at Meadville Lombard

---

103 David Pohl, "To Respond, to Engage, to Celebrate, to Challenge," sermon at General Assembly sponsored by SLM, Hollywood, Florida, June 1991.

104 Barbara Child, "The Society for the Larger Ministry: A History of Impassioned Vision Brought to Life," in *Community Ministry: An Opportunity for Renewal and Change—A Report on Research and Reflection* (Starr King Community Ministry Project, 1995).

105 This was accomplished by amending Article VII, Section 7.6 of the UUA bylaws.

Theological School. After the 1991 bylaw change, Gerdes applied for community ministry credentials as minister librarian and educator. "I saw this as an important designation for myself; I also wanted to give it more credence, some legitimacy."[106] Ralph Mero saw the third track of ministry as an opportunity to restore the official ministerial status he had lost when he left parish ministry. He sent a letter to the Department of Ministry detailing his work as Director of Planned Parenthood of Seattle and was soon grand-parented in as a community minister. Now he was recognized for his work with Planned Parenthood and with Compassion in Dying, which he had founded as one of the nation's first "right-to-die" organizations.

Scott Giles was ordained to ministry in 1978 and served as a parish minister from 1978 to 1991. He also became a Board Certified Chaplain specializing in hypnosis in the treatment of pain. When the UU community ministry track was added, he was grand-parented in for his work as a chaplain without having to go through preliminary fellowship. "The community ministry designation was liberating for me," he states.[107]

Michelle Bentley was grand-parented into fellowship as a community minister in 1996. As an African-American woman, she had been involved in community work long before being ordained into parish ministry in 1986. Bentley walked a dual path of ministry— serving, alternately and together, ministries in both parish and community settings in inner-city Chicago. The importance of Bentley's work is underscored by the UUA's 1994 Urban Church Profile. This report described the "high population density, economic distress, middle-class flight, crime, unemployment, low education levels, and family and cultural breakdown" that characterize inner city neighborhoods.[108] To bring healing and possibility into situations such as this has been central to the vision of Bentley's ministry.

New community ministries also surfaced during this time.

Cheng Imm Tan was one of the first to be ordained under the new track of community ministry. She and Peter Thoms chose to be ordained not by any one church, but rather by twenty-eight of

---

106 Neil Gerdes, interview with Kathleen Parker, August 2004.
107 See the website for the Rev. Dr. Scott Giles, www.counselingministries.com.
108 "Urban UU: History of the Urban Ministry Efforts of the UUA."

the congregations that were members of the UU Urban Ministry (formerly the Benevolent Fraternity) of Boston. In 1982 Tan began work as an intern at Renewal House, an emergency shelter for battered women, founded in 1978 by the Rev. Elizabeth Ellis-Hagler as a program of the Benevolent Fraternity.[109] At Renewal House Tan created space for Chinese, Vietnamese, and Cambodian women. The lack of multicultural services and understanding, Tan would later say, meant that "Asian women were forced to face their batterers over and over again."[110] Today Tan is head of New Bostonians, a program to assist immigrant populations in Boston with economic, social, and cultural needs. She also directs Gund Kwok, a martial arts Asian women's lion and dragon dance troupe. The fact that women are the dancers, instead of men, is personally empowering for them and speaks metaphorically to Tan's twenty-year life in community ministry.

José Ballester became a Unitarian Universalist in 1979, attracted to the movement by the Universalist message of hope. In 1992 Steve Shick hired Ballester to work with the Just Works program at the Unitarian Universalist Service Committee. Ballester drew on the model of Universalist work camps to design innovative programs bringing young people and adults into direct relationship with people in severe poverty.[111] In that capacity, he was able to combine religious education and community ministry and bring both to people in congregations.

David Pettee entered Starr King School for the Ministry in 1985. From the beginning, he was certain that his call to ministry was not toward the parish but toward a larger service. He was one of four Starr King students who took a leave of absence in 1985 to walk with the Great Peace March for Global Nuclear Disarmament.[112] The passage of the 1991 bylaw change for community ministry prompted Pettee to begin his preparation for ministerial fellowship. He com-

---

109 Neil Chethik, "Outside Church Walls," *UU World* September/October 1994, 19.

110 Cheng Imm Tan, "Building Inclusive Cities and What That Demands of Us," sermon delivered at the UUA Continental Conference on Urban Ministries, March 11, 2001, as reported by Deborah Weiner, "Urban Church Conference Participants Celebrate Sunday Worship at Peoples Church in Chicago." See www.uua.org/urbanuu/urbanministriesconference/sunworship.html.

111 Jose Ballester, interview with Dorothy Emerson, August 10, 2005.

112 See http://www.uua.org/actions/peace/85march.html.

pleted a year-long hospital chaplaincy, successfully interviewed with the Ministerial Fellowship Committee in 1993, and soon after that took a full-time hospice position with the Visiting Nurses Association (VNA). In 1994, he was ordained to community ministry—the first in the Pacific Central District—by the First Unitarian Universalist Church of San Francisco, which endorsed his hospice ministry. While there, he also served as minister-in-residence at Starr King and taught a course in community ministry.

In 2002, Pettee accepted a position with the UUA as Ministerial Credentialing Director. He brought his experience as a community minister to the credentialing position in Boston. He reflects, "I have been in conversation on community ministry for twenty years; others have been in it longer than I. The earlier challenges deeply imprinted feelings of marginality and estrangement for many, but I believe there have been dramatic changes since 1991."[113]

In fact, the 1991 decision to grant official recognition to community ministers inaugurated a long process of assessment and accommodation. Community ministers wanted their ministries to be granted equal and official standing by the Ministerial Fellowship Committee; they also wanted acceptance among their peers in the UU Ministers Association. The chief institutional difficulty lay in the fact that the Unitarian tradition, more so than the Universalist tradition, had generally tied ministry to a particular congregation, which served to confer ordination and provide compensation.[114] In community ministry, the role of the congregation, or its absence, posed a central question needing to be resolved.

In 1995, Daniel Hotchkiss, a staff member in the Department of Ministry, prepared a statement to the UUA Department of Ministry that, Neil Shadle recalled, raised "some sharp intelligent questions."[115] To successfully implement the 1991 bylaw change, Hotchkiss believed the UUA would need, among other things, to develop a common theory by which to structure community ministry

---

113 David Pettee, interview with Kathleen Parker, July 8, 2005.

114 The chief exceptions to this pattern are found in the ordination of ministers by the Benevolent Fraternity in the 1830s; Charles Barnard and Frederick T. Gray became ministers-at-large to the Benevolent Fraternity in 1834. Also, throughout the nineteenth century, the AUA recognized the ministerial standing of presidents of Harvard Divinity School who had previously served as Unitarian ministers.

115 Neil Shadle, interview with Kathleen Parker, August 19, 2004.

within the existing framework of ministry. How would the idea of ministry as a mutual covenant between a leader and followers be adapted to community ministry, where the "followers are more diffuse and unlikely to engage in a covenant?"[116] He then offered, "If a congregation is ordaining a community minister, it is the congregation's social mission that the minister is charged to help fulfill." He promoted the idea that community ministers might fulfill the historical congregational relationship by maintaining "an institutional tie to a congregation, District, UUA affiliate, or to the UUA itself." [117]

Shortly after the Hotchkiss paper came out, Shipley worked with the newly formed Community Ministry Council in the Pacific Central District to formulate guidelines for the affiliation of community ministers with congregations. Shipley urged community ministers to tie their work to congregations and to see how their ministry could be inherited by succeeding generations.[118] With assistance from a series of grants, the Pacific Central District produced several versions of a spiral-bound book, *Guidelines for the Affiliation of Community Clergy with Unitarian Universalist Congregations*. This resource helped many community ministers and congregations to develop written agreements defining their relationships with each other.[119]

Leslie Westbrook served on the Ministerial Fellowship Committee from 1996 to 2003.[120] Reflecting on her experience, she witnessed this same concern and outcome: "The MFC wanted to recognize people working in the community, but it also wanted to support the congregations."[121]

---

116 Daniel Hotchkiss, "Defining Community Ministry," unpublished paper to the UUA Department of Ministry, 1996.

117 Note that Hotchkiss's recommendation included the possibility of affiliation with UUA affiliate organizations, while the rule set by the MFC in 1992 allowed affiliation only with associate member organizations. There are three such organizations: the UU Women's Federation, the UU Service Committee, and the UU-United Nations Office.

118 Patty Franz, interview with Kathleen Parker, June 19, 2005.

119 Patty Franz, interview with Kathleen Parker, July 21, 2005.

120 Westbrook, it will be recalled, served as UUA staff person on the Women and Religion Committee from 1978 to 1981. Ordained to parish ministry in 1973, she was credentialed in community ministry in 1991.

121 Leslie Westbrook, interview with Kathleen Parker, June 29, 2005.

INSTITUTIONAL CHANGES AND DEVELOPMENTS

As community ministries emerged after 1991, a lot of institutional connections were being made behind the scenes. SLM leadership focused on building the institutional base for community ministry, working with the UUA, the Ministerial Fellowship Committee, and the UU Ministers Association (UUMA) to adopt policies that would include community ministers. At the 1994 General Assembly in Fort Worth, Neil Shadle gave the James Reeb Memorial Lecture on "Community Ministry and the True Church of Democracy." After thirty years of doing urban ministry and teaching courses in community ministry at Meadville Lombard, Shadle powerfully outlined the need for a democratic vision of religion in a pluralistic society. The church should not be a private enclave; it should be a steward of public life. We must be interfaith to do this, he said, even as we are interracial and intercultural.

A critical point of institutional cooperation took place with the convening of the Consultation on Community Ministry, held in Boston, March 1–3, 1996.[122] Planned by the SLM Steering Committee and the UUA Board Ministry Working Group, representatives from twelve different constituencies participated in the Consultation.[123] Steve Shick came to the Consultation thinking it would be good to get all these interests around the table to promote community ministry. In particular, he "wanted to see some clarity, because already there was talk of doing away with the three separate tracks of ministry." Shick hoped that the Consultation would put an end to the idea of discontinuing the separate tracks. There was satisfaction that the third track provided an official necessary place of ministerial recognition, but concern also that the three separate tracks artificially restricted one's preparation for fuller ministerial service. In 1995, a report from the Starr King Community Ministry Project had ques-

---

122 Although the UUA Board agreed to the Consultation, it was held "at no cost to the UUA" and was supported by an additional grant SLM received for this purpose. In addition, the UUMA contributed funds to cover their participation.

123 Groups represented at the consultation included SLM, the UUA Board and Staff, the Ministerial Fellowship Committee, the Commission on Appraisal, the UU theological schools, the UUMA, African American and Latino/a UU ministers, and the UUSC.

tioned whether "a splintered and fragmented approach to ministry" would properly "embody the wholeness we seek to support in society."[124] The recommendations of the 1996 Consultation placed before the board of the UUA included a proposal to establish a UUA Commission on Community Ministry that would "create a long-term plan for community ministries to include a wider vision of ministry for the denomination" and "establish a staff structure" to meet the needs of community ministries.[125]

Meanwhile, the question that worried Steve Shick—whether to dissolve the three tracks of ministry into one—had in fact been reopened. In 1995, the UU Ministers Association Executive Committee had conducted an informal survey of its members and found support for instituting a single category of ministry.[126] In 1997, the Commission on Appraisal reported, "Ministers should be received into Ministerial Fellowship with the potential for adding areas of specialization." After the UUMA passed a resolution in 1999 proposing a new structure for categories, a Task Force on Categories was convened, including members of the Ministerial Fellowship Committee, the UUMA, and the UUA Board of Trustees. By September 2000, the MFC voted affirmatively for the second time on the motion "that preliminary fellowship will be granted in ministry without regard to category."

Unfortunately, at this same time, the Society for the Larger Ministry fell into a period of inactivity, and its newsletter *Crossroads* ceased publication from 1996 to 1999. The reasons were many. There was disappointment that Skinner House had declined to publish the manuscript, "The Challenge of Right Relationship: Community Ministry and Unitarian Universalism," which had been developed out of the 1995 Starr King report.[127] There was concern that the pro-

---

124 "Community Ministry: An Opportunity for Renewal and Change," Starr King Community Ministry Project, 1995. Authors listed as Barbara Child, Jeanne Clemons, Gail Collins-Randive, Tawna Nicholas Cooley, Alicia Forsey, Mary Harrington, and Rebecca Parker, with Kyle Nash for the final conversation, 6.

125 "Recommendations from the Consultation on Community Ministry to the Board of Trustees of the Unitarian Universalist Association," March 1–3, 1996.

126 This history is described in "A Draft Proposal to Redesign Fellowship for Unitarian Universalist Ministry," March 2004, reviewed and amended April 2004.

127 This was an early collection of essays written by community ministers, funded by a grant from UUSC and edited by Barbara Jo Sorenson and Joan Engel. As an unpublished manuscript, it continued to provide a source of information and inspiration among community ministers.

posals of the 1996 Consultation on Community Ministry in Boston had led to no tangible results. There was a leadership vacuum, with new leaders failing to emerge when the founders moved on.[128] On a personal level, many community ministers were reportedly experiencing burnout or inadequate financial support in their respective areas of work.[129] Finally, there was an increasing sense of confusion over proposals at the UUA and MFC to fold the three tracks of ministry into one.

Many community ministers found an ally in Jody Shipley. "Jody held the banner high, even when nothing was happening," stated Maddie Sifantus. Though she maintained a sometimes-interrupted parish ministry for twenty-six years, Shipley continued her ministry to community ministers. To facilitate communication, she started a community ministry e-mail list that initially served the Pacific Central District but eventually expanded into a national and international network. In 1998, she founded the Unitarian Universalist Community Ministry Center in Berkeley. The Center was set up as a non-profit organization, with a small, mostly local board of directors that could focus on programs in the San Francisco Bay Area. Many describe the Center as Shipley's personal ministry. It was essentially an organization through which she could combine all her community ministries—writing grant proposals, holding conferences, running retreats, and offering educational workshops.

At General Assembly in 1998, a group of community ministers began to meet again to determine what might be done to address their concerns and revive the Society for the Larger Ministry.[130] In November 1999 *Crossroads* resumed publication with a grant from the Unitarian Universalist Ministers Association. In the first issue, Shipley announced that after several years of silence, "we [again] crank up this organization...everything is cold...a little misplaced... but we're underway."[131] SLM resumed offering yearly community ministry workshops at General Assembly, and the membership of

---

128 Dorothy Emerson, interview with Kathleen Parker, August 18, 2005.

129 Stephen Shick, interview with Kathleen Parker, August 3, 2005.

130 Those meeting to revive SLM included Steve Schick, Judy Morris, Linnea Pearson, Jody Shipley, and Marilyn Gentile, according to a promotional flyer, 2000.

131 Jody Shipley, "Under the Golden Arches," *Crossroads*, newsletter of the Society for the Larger Ministry, November 24, 1999.

SLM climbed to eighty. Shipley had stepped in as the driving force, but she knew that others needed to assume longer-term leadership. She also wanted to focus more of her time and energy on the UU Community Ministry Center she had founded in Berkeley. With her recommendation in 2001, Jeanne Lloyd and Maddie Sifantus took over as the co-chairs of SLM, with Shipley as the treasurer.

Community ministers still felt the need for parity with parish ministers, and the MFC proposal for one ministry track appeared as a setback in the matter of parity. When the proposal to merge the separate tracks of ministry came up at the March 2002 Ministers Convocation in Birmingham, Alabama, the ensuing discussion led to a heated debate. As a result, community ministers met at the Convocation and decided to establish a Community Ministry Focus Group (CMFG) to advocate for community ministers within the UUMA.[132] With an eye to creating a culture as well as a structure that would support and affirm community ministers and their work, the Steering Committee engaged in dialogue with both the UUMA leadership and the community ministers in the field.

A meeting of the Community Ministry Focus Group was held the following June at Ministry Days prior to General Assembly, immediately preceding a special public meeting of the UUMA Committee on Categories. Community ministers who attended that meeting expressed their concerns about the lack of inclusive process by which decisions were being made regarding their status and about continuing inequities among different categories of ministers. The UUMA Committee on Categories listened and subsequently recommended to the Ministerial Fellowship Committee and the UUMA Executive Committee that the process of merging the tracks be slowed down. More input and greater consensus was needed before proceeding.

With the formation of the UUMA Community Ministry Focus Group, there were then three community ministry organizations, the other two being the Society for the Larger Ministry and the UU Community Ministry Center. Considered weak in organizational

---

132 The Community Ministry Focus Group (CMFG) would function like the focus group already in place for ministers of religious education. Because it came out of the UUMA, the CMFG did not include lay ministers. The initial Steering Committee included Roger Brewin, Dorothy Emerson, Anita Farber-Robertson, Ann Galloway-Edge, Jeanne Lloyd, Bonnie Meyer, Suzanne Owens-Pike, Deborah Pope-Lance, and Jody Shipley.

skills, Jody Shipley had nonetheless been central to the development of all three groups. Her strengths, as many have attested, lay in her pastoral care of community ministers and in her ability to serve as a catalyst for community ministry organizing and advocacy. She was awarded the SLM "Community Minister of the Year Award" at the 2002 General Assembly but was unable to attend to receive the award. Sadly, Shipley had become gravely ill with lymphoma. Her death in October 2002 was a blow to everyone who had looked to her for leadership and left the separate community ministry organizations with a need to take stock. How would they now be run, by whom, and for what purpose?

The need for clarity led representatives from the three organizations to apply for a special grant for a Community Ministry Summit, to be held the day after General Assembly 2003 in Boston.[133] Community minister Nancy Bowen was engaged to facilitate the process of planning and conducting the Summit. She asked each of the three community ministry organizations to prepare a "concept paper" describing: (1) their group's mission; (2) the attributes that made their group unique; (3) their key accomplishments; and (4) their points of confusion about identity, funding, and accountability. Among the thirty people who attended the Summit, there were many who came with allegiances to more than one group. All came with the idea of advancing community ministry through cooperative efforts. In addition to representatives of the three community ministry groups, representatives from the UUMA, UUA Board of Trustees, and UUA staff also participated. David Hubner, then director of the UUA Ministerial and Professional Leadership Staff Group (formerly the Department of Ministry), recalled that there was a lot to work through. "There was grief work to be done over the loss of Jody Shipley. There were also struggles over competing visions and strategies of leadership. It was hard to sort out who to listen to and easy to lose heart in the process."[134]

---

133 Jeanne Lloyd from SLM, Dorothy Emerson from CMFG, and Margie McCue from UUCMC were joined by Maddie Sifantus from both SLM and UUCMC in forming the Planning Committee. Dorothy Emerson wrote the grant proposal to the Fund for Unitarian Universalism. SLM was the fiscal agent. Nancy Bowen served as the facilitator, beginning in March 2003, working with the Planning Committee and continuing after the Summit to facilitate the Coalition.

134 David Hubner, interview with Kathleen Parker, July 21, 2005.

Nancy Bowen prepared a report on the Summit revealing the frank honesty with which participants looked at the current reality of community ministry—its strengths and weaknesses as well as its benefits and dangers. Strengths included a sense of call, passion, diverse skills, good will, and an entrepreneurial spirit; weaknesses included over-commitment, murky vision, competitiveness, a lone-ranger stereotype, and whining. Acknowledging this last weakness brought laughter and the recognition that it was time to stop whining and move forward with a common vision.

Key decisions made at the summit were to establish a committee to facilitate communication among the organizations, research and prepare a book on community ministry,[135] develop an educational program for parish ministers to learn about community ministry, and develop a manual of community ministry guidelines. At the end of the day, David Hubner "took the bold step...to volunteer his office to serve as an ex-officio member of what would later become the Community Ministry Coalition."[136] The creation of the Community Ministry Coalition was perhaps the most significant outcome of the Summit. More than anything, it marked an opening up of dialogue and cooperation between the separate and overlapping community ministry entities, with the UUA as a full partner in that conversation.[137]

Already under way was a proposal to incorporate SLM as a non-profit organization, in the hope that this status would promote greater legitimacy, stability, and accountability. After a year of meetings among the members of the Coalition, the San Francisco–based UU Community Ministry Center proposed to fold its vision and mission into that of SLM. Then, in December 2004, the membership of the Society for the Larger Ministry voted to change its name to the Unitarian Universalist Society for Community Ministries (UUSCM). The name change affirmed the group's focus on community ministry and at the same time eliminated the recurring name confusion

---

135 The initial grant for the present book had been received from the Fund for Unitarian Universalism just prior to the Summit. Dorothy Emerson wrote the proposal. SLM had agreed to serve as the fiscal agent.

136 Jeanne Lloyd, e-mail to Kathleen Parker, Dorothy Emerson, Maddie Sifantus, David Pettee, and Ralph Mero, June 30, 2005.

137 David Pettee, interview with Kathleen Parker, July 8, 2005.

between SLM and the Church of the Larger Fellowship.[138] In January 2005, Kurt Kuhwald, formerly a board member for the Center, joined the board of UUSCM and was named Director of Education to carry on the continuing mission of the Center within UUSCM.[139]

To create a stronger organizational structure and foster the development of new leadership, Jeanne Lloyd and Maddie Sifantus, who had served first as co-chairs and then as co-presidents of SLM, altered their leadership roles. In 2005 Lloyd became president, and Sifantus became vice president, of the renamed Society for Community Ministries. The nonprofit status of UUSCM was finalized in June 2005. Now donors could claim a tax deduction, making it easier for the organization to attract funding. UUSCM focused on reaching out to its membership through better communication, using their website. The site provides information about UUSCM, its goals, organizational developments, the issues and events it is working on, and the work of individual community ministers.[140] Community ministers are invited to post descriptions of their work and a statement of the covenant they maintain with a congregation or other organization endorsing their ministry. In addition, the website includes the Code of Professional Practice developed by and for members, both lay and clergy. Now recognized as a UUA Professional Organization, UUSCM has created the infrastructure to support its expanded vision, role, and purpose.

Since the Summit of 2003, community ministry has come into a place of greater visibility and acceptance within the institutional structures of the UUA. It is encouraging that a number of ordained and fellowshipped community ministers serve in leadership positions at the UUA. In 2008, these community ministers included Bill Sinkford, President of the UUA; David Pettee, Director of Ministerial Credentialing; and Ralph Mero, Director of Church Staff Finances. In addition, as Beth Miller, then Director of Ministry and Professional Leadership, pointed out, "All ordained folks at the UUA essentially serve as community ministers."

---

138 Church of the Larger Fellowship is a Unitarian Universalist congregation with members all over the world, originally connected by mail and increasingly now via the Internet.
139 See the UUSCM Annual Report, FYE June 30, 2005.
140 Jeanne Lloyd, interview with Kathleen Parker, March 22, 2005.

David Hubner, as we have seen, was "instrumental in raising up community ministry in the UUA and helping it find parity in fellowship, practice, and process."[141] Hubner believed that "community ministry offers a kind of creativity and entrepreneurial spirit that is visionary. It is also of enormous value to congregations because it helps shift the sense of ministry to engage with the world."[142] And finally, there is a movement under way to recognize and credential at some level the gifts and commitments of lay community ministers.

In regard to the issue of separate tracks for ministry, as of its September 2005 meeting, the Ministerial Fellowship Committee agreed it would no longer ask candidates to indicate which category of ministry they planned to pursue and began granting preliminary fellowship to UU ministers on the premise that all candidates should be prepared to serve in any ministerial capacity.[143] For many, this decision makes real a flexibility and wholeness in ministry that is desirable and already being practiced. Others fear it will fragment or attenuate preparation for ministry that could otherwise be focused on the community ministry they plan to pursue.

The flow of people answering the call to community ministry continues.[144] Lee Barker, President and Professor of Ministry at Meadville Lombard Theological School, described the change in how students view ministry. "Less than a generation ago, students took up their studies with nearly a single-minded understanding of ministry. These days, students appear on our campus with a different expanded understanding of the possibilities for ministry."[145] Beth Miller explained her approach to serving the growing number of community ministers emerging in our movement: "As I and the rest of Ministry and Professional Leadership staff visit seminaries, talk with students, and see people come through the [credentialing process], it is clear that the call to ministry beyond the congregational

---

141 Lloyd, e-mail to Parker, June 2005.

142 David Hubner, interview with Kathleen Parker, July 21, 2005.

143 David Pettee, interview with Kathleen Parker, July 7, 2005. The General Assembly was not involved in this decision, because it did not involve a bylaw change, and the UUA Board had empowered the MFC to resolve the question. Wayne Arneson, interview with Kathleen Parker, July 13, 2005.

144 David Pettee estimates that about 40 percent of incoming ministerial students are interested in community ministry, and that about 16 percent will choose community ministry as their specialty.

145 Lee Barker, Foreword, in Parker, *Sacred Service in Civic Space*, ix.

context is powerful for many people. We have not served these ministers, the institutions and organizations they serve, or the congregations they relate to, as well as we might." [146] To address this need, Robin Tanner, a seminarian at Harvard Divinity School, was hired for two years as a part-time intern to help get a clear picture of who the fellowshipped community ministers were, where they were serving, what needs they felt the UUA might serve to support their ministries and their relationships with Unitarian Universalism. Miller stated, "My hope is that this project will be the beginning of a much more intentional, supportive, and mutually beneficial relationship with our community ministers and those they serve."

The following words from the 1995 Report of the Starr King Community Ministry Project ought not be lost to history. "The community ministry movement places our congregations within a larger sense of mission...to begin with an affirmation of the sacred power present in all of life."[147] Carefully and prophetically, this report gives witness to the historic importance of community ministry in this time. "Something worthwhile is stirring within our religious movement," observed the authors. Then, expectantly and prayerfully, they added, "Let it rise on wings."

And so it has. The organizational healing and focus that came about with the Community Ministry Summit affirmed that sense of prophecy and possibility—for the life of our institution, our ministries, and our work in the world.

---

146 Beth Miller, e-mail to Dorothy Emerson, November 21, 2007.

147 "Community Ministry: An Opportunity for Renewal and Change," (San Francisco: Starr King Community Ministry Project, 1995).

IV. STORIES
OF CONTEMPORARY
COMMUNITY MINISTRY

In the moving story that follows, Anita Farber-Robertson draws an analogy between the individual blocks of a quilt, designed and constructed for a dying woman by friends separated by distance, and the unique nature of individual community ministries, which together become a kaleidoscope of intention and care. This prepares the reader for the compelling individual accounts of community ministry, gathered through oral testimony and retold with sensitivity by Mary Ganz. They include the Faithful Fools Street Ministry in the Tenderloin district of San Francisco, chaplaincies in numerous settings, administrative ministries in the UUA, Donald Robinson's ministry with youth through Beacon House in Washington, DC, Jim Cavenaugh's prison ministry, and many others. Together they provide a rich record of the powerful work being done by those who are "called to community."

AN INTRODUCTION

by the Rev. Dr. Anita Farber-Robertson

I had finished conducting worship in the small village church. Wendy was lingering. She was in a bit of distress.

"What's the matter, Wendy?" I asked.

Her eyes filled up as she told me of her childhood friend who was losing her battle with cancer. Cathy and their friends were scattered across the country. Wanting Cathy to feel the love and care in which she was held, Wendy had come up with a plan.

Wendy sent a letter to all of Cathy's family and friends, asking each person to construct a square that in some way represented their care and appreciation of Cathy. Wendy would collect the squares, sew them together into a quilt, and send it down to Cathy, who would then be wrapped in their love.

With Cathy's health deteriorating, Wendy worried that it would not reach completion in time. She waited for the last of the squares, which were to be twelve-inches square, "with maybe a touch of red to signify Cathy's courage" she had told them. She had invited people to do whatever they liked—embroider, cut and stitch, or just write something with permanent marker, only to do it soon and send it to her. This broke all the quilting rules I had ever learned. But I knew that wasn't the point.

The next day Wendy called. The last of the squares had arrived. She had worked into the night to put these mismatched and incredibly different squares together. The next day she sewed it all onto a huge piece of backing, wrapped it up, and sent it via Overnight Delivery. She e-mailed me a picture of the quilt hanging on a line under the sun.

More than beautiful, it was a testimony to human love and tenderness, and to the power of the heart to overcome the suffering of the soul. It shimmered. Despite the fact that it did not adhere to any rules of consistency of fabric, construction, content, or style, as a whole it told a story no single piece could have conveyed.

Cathy's quilt captured how it is that human community congeals in the midst of diversity and even disparity. We present here the word-picture quilt of community ministry as it looks today. Unlike Wendy, we could not include everybody. But we believe we have included enough diversity of ministries, which people have crafted, that when you step back and grasp the whole, you too will see a testimony to human love and tenderness, and to the power of the heart to overcome the suffering of the soul. It shimmers.

COMMUNITY MINISTRIES MADE REAL: SNAPSHOTS FROM 2005[148]

by the Rev. Mary McKinnon Ganz

It was a bright, sunny, San Francisco afternoon, hot enough to wear sleeveless dresses and short-sleeve shirts and sip wine on an apartment balcony while pasta bubbled on the stove. The apartment was tiny, clean, and bright. The host beamed as his friends exclaimed their approval of his new home and their joy to be together.

The coffee table and TV were freebies. He had bought the sofa and the bed. A friend had scavenged a computer and promised to get it working soon. And on the wall was framed a familiar sign, hand-painted on cardboard:

> ABDUCTED BY ALIENS
> MISSED MY DINNER
> HELP IF YOU CAN
> THANK YOU

This was the sign Bruce had used to beg for change for the last several of the thirty-one years he'd lived on the streets. Nearly every day, he had stood next to the grave of Thomas Starr King at the corner of Franklin Street and Starr King Way, flashing that sign at motorists stopped at the light. He was well known to members of the First Unitarian Universalist Society of San Francisco, not only for his presence on their corner but for his terrifying outbursts—directed sometimes at church members or church staff who didn't have change for him that day, or who offered him food he didn't like.

Present on his new balcony that June afternoon were several of the ministers who had kept faith with Bruce over nine months of patient walking and reflecting, asking always, "What keeps us separate? What connects us?" They had accompanied Bruce as he struggled to get off of heroin and onto methadone, and then off methadone. And

---

148 Please note that this section of the book was completed in 2008 and reflects the ministries people were engaged in at the time. Some of these ministries have changed.

they had shown up with him again and again in a protracted court battle to get Social Security Disability Income for his HIV-positive and dual-diagnosis mental-health status. They had helped him look for an apartment and had stood up for him when questions arose about his lengthy criminal record.

This is one of the faces of community ministry in the twenty-first century—the community of lay and ordained ministers from the Faithful Fools Street Ministry, walking with people like Bruce, and walking also with people from the San Francisco hillsides and suburbs who are trying to get out of their own mental cages and look at poverty in a new way.

Community ministries today take many forms, and most embody more than one of the several types of ministry: prophetic, pastoral, educational, administrative, and priestly. On any day, coast to coast and around the world, one might find UU community ministers:

- Holding the hand of a sick person in the hospital or home hospice
- Sitting in a broom closet on an aircraft carrier, next to a young man whose life or work in the military is overwhelming him in this moment
- Helping young residents of a housing project with their math problems at an after-school program
- Coaching an individual to figure out "next steps" for her life
- Writing an op-ed piece about mental health issues
- Leading a community chorus, or digging with youth in a community garden
- Teaching life skills to women in prison
- Crafting a public statement on behalf of the denomination in response to an opening on the US Supreme Court

It is tempting to tell you about every different and meaningful community ministry of which we are aware. It would take several volumes, so much good ministry is happening. What we have chosen to do here is to offer snapshots capturing different folk in their work and showing part of the journey it took to get there. When you are finished, the pictures as a whole will, much like Cathy's healing friendship quilt, suggest the depth, the texture, and incredible richness of the community ministry flourishing in our midst.

Often community ministry can be seen most clearly not in the face of an individual minister but in the shape of a community of empowerment coming into being. The Faithful Fools is such a community.

THE FAITHFUL FOOLS STREET MINISTRY: SAN FRANCISCO; MANAGUA, NICARAGUA; VANCOUVER, BRITISH COLUMBIA; RICHMOND, CALIFORNIA

It began with one person, walking.

The Rev. Dr. **Kay Jorgensen** landed in San Francisco in 1995 after seven years in a Minnesota parish, answering a call from the streets that she had first heard as a mime and a clown doing street theater. "I began walking the streets of the Tenderloin—every day, just walking," Jorgensen said. She would begin at the steps of the First Unitarian Universalist Society of San Francisco, opening a walking path between the church and the Tenderloin, separated by only a few downhill blocks—and by chasms of privilege and power. "I was cleaning houses to survive," Jorgensen said, "and I began to see that there was a ministry here."

Jorgensen became social action chair at the San Francisco church, building a social justice ministry that sought to connect people in the parish with people in the community. In 1999, with some support from the Unitarian Universalist Veatch Program at Shelter Rock, the congregation voted her as social justice minister.

Meanwhile, she continued to walk. Just as it became clear to Jorgensen that there was potential for more ministry on the streets than she could do alone, she met Sr. Carmen Barsody, OSF, of the Franciscan Sisters of Little Falls, Minnesota. Barsody had returned from a mission in Nicaragua, where she had practiced a "ministry of presence" that matched what Jorgensen was doing in the Tenderloin.

In 1998, Jorgensen and Barsody adopted the name "Faithful Fools," hearkening back to Jorgensen's experience as a clown and Barsody's experience as a follower of St. Francis, whom others called a "fool for God." Fools are truth-tellers, too—the ones who can speak truth to the king and keep their heads.

They began holding street retreats out of the San Francisco UU church.

Street retreats offer an opportunity for people from churches, youth groups, and other communities of relative affluence to have an authentic encounter with the poverty that exists in the center of San Francisco, in the midst of a city of great wealth. Within seven years of the founding of the Fools, more than 1,300 people had been guided to wander several hours through the Tenderloin, to stand in line for a meal at Glide Church or St. Anthony's Dining Hall, and to pay attention to the assumptions and the feelings that arise within them while they are doing it.

Street retreats remain a staple of the community's practice. Like Jorgensen's solitary walks, they begin at the UU church, located atop Cathedral Hill, an historic symbol of civic and economic power. From there Jorgensen and Barsody led the way downhill to the Tenderloin, where the Faithful Fools are located in a purple-painted building that serves as Jorgensen's and Barsody's home, as the location of a local copy shop, and as community space for the many programs of the Fools or other groups. At the end of the day, those on retreat gather in the spacious community room upstairs—"Fools' Court"— to share their experiences: the pain and joy of their encounters in the Tenderloin.

On other days, the space may be in use for arts programs, including drama workshops, monthly poetry readings, a film series, or for community gatherings, including a weekly Bible study in which some members have been reading scripture together for twenty years. Or it may be occupied by people editing a poetry anthology or chatting over tea and coffee after daily meditation in the "street zendo" downstairs.

Every year, some members of the community of lay and professional ministers make an extended street retreat, sleeping on the streets or in shelters for as long as seven nights. Each year, also,

Jorgensen and Barsody have led some of the people who have completed an overnight street retreat—thus grounding them in poverty in this country—to Nicaragua, where they are guests of families living in barrios in Managua. The Faithful Fools now have acquired a building in Managua and opened "Fools' Court of the South," which is in use year-round as a gathering place by the community.

"The Fools are a place of learning, of open invitation," Barsody said. "Many ministers and seminarians come to learn and work and discover the space between the parish and the community. Sometimes they come to be here in the Tenderloin for a while and then go to a parish or other ministry, but they keep working with the fool mind, the fool consciousness."

The Rev. **Kurt Kuhwald** is one of the second-generation ministers at the Faithful Fools, one who came out of a parish and held open the possibility of returning to parish ministry. Kuhwald's interest in the Faithful Fools began with a growing feeling that he needed to do ministry with people who are oppressed and marginalized. Jorgensen suggested he make a street retreat.

"I thought, sure, this would be a helpful thing in directing me to get a sense of what I could do, what kind of path I could take," Kuhwald said. "So I took a street retreat, and in the first hour—no, within *minutes*—I felt this great sensation like I had come home, and I was in the right place. This was my community, these were my people, this was my work."

At the end of the year, he moved into an apartment in the Tenderloin and began working part-time with the Faithful Fools, while continuing to do a part-time consulting ministry with a congregation in northern California. The following year he sought endorsement as a community minister with the San Francisco church and began a ministry of grant writing, advocacy, and pulpit supply preaching about homelessness, poverty, and the Faithful Fools, in addition to general support for the work of the ministry. One of his roles was to travel to UU churches and other community groups that were exploring and supporting street ministry by staging *The Witness*.

The Witness is a play about the experience of a street retreat as told by a young woman. As he watched it again and again, the lines began to sink into Kuhwald's being. "You know," he said one day to

Martha Boesing, the playwright, "this play ought to be rewritten for a man."

Boesing mulled that over for at least a year before she came to Kuhwald and said, "You're right. And I want you to be the actor."

Kuhwald had never acted before, and suddenly he was memorizing lines for a single-actor production, playing several roles. The lead was now a middle-aged man who discovers a new way to be with himself and the world through his tearing aside the veil of separation during a street retreat.

Reflecting on this unexpected turn his ministry had taken, Kuhwald said, "That's the issue of being open to the unknown; you really are an entrepreneur. There is no model for it. What we typically think of as ministries is: you pastor, you preach, you teach. For most of us to think about walking out of that model causes nothing but terror."

Kuhwald is not altogether comfortable with the word *entrepreneur* but hasn't found a better one to describe the work of cobbling together ministries that he finds himself doing. "It's clear to me now that what I need to be doing is creating an independent ministry, a ministry I am fully responsible for guiding," he said.

He is one of a group of several community and parish ministers who participate in a monthly conference call as part of the Faithful Fools' "New Ministry Incubator Project," designed to support ministers who are working to create ministries authentic to their sense of call. These conferences give ministers a chance to check in about the progress of building their ministries by assessing issues and bringing roadblocks to the group. "We need to be asking each other questions on what is the meaning of our ministry," Jorgensen said.

Those deep questions are part of the everyday work of the Faithful Fools, which uses the action-reflection-action model of Brazilian educator Paulo Friere. "So much of our experience gets lost, truly lost, and we don't make time to integrate it," Jorgensen said. "The reflection has to be as strong as the action. And that's hard to do, because we're so action-oriented."

Through the years, Jorgensen has supervised interns at the San Francisco church and at the Faithful Fools, and has mentored seminarians in a class, "Bearing Witness," which she and Barsody have taught at Starr King School for the Ministry. Some of Jorgensen's former interns, like the Rev. **Karen Day**, went on to parishes, where they brought a community ministry consciousness; others, such as the Rev. **Barbara Meyers** of Fremont, began their own community ministries; and one, **Laura Friedman**, began street retreats and other programs inspired by the Faithful Fools in Vancouver, BC. Meanwhile **Denis Paul**, a Starr King seminarian and member of the San Francisco UU church, began street retreats in a poverty-stricken area of Richmond, California, involving members and ministers of the "church on the hill" nearest to that area, First Unitarian Universalist Church of Berkeley, located in Kensington.

As the San Francisco church entered search for new parish ministry, Jorgensen announced her retirement from her staff position as social justice minister, to create space for the congregation and the Search Committee to "study the role of social justice in the overall life of the congregation and determine its significance for the future." Jorgensen would remain an affiliated community minister, in covenant with the congregation for her ministry at the Faithful Fools.

"What we've done in social justice has sprung from the heart of our liberal religious faith, and that's grounded in the congregation," Jorgensen said. "It's not something that will come and go."

As the program strength has grown, the Faithful Fools Street Ministry has become what Jorgensen called a "locus of possibility": an open space where ministries may be born out of people's deep yearning—such as Kuhwald's surprising venture into expressing his own community ministry through acting. And as the Faithful Fools have grown institutionally, Jorgensen and Barsody have become sharply aware how easily the busyness of institution-tending can crowd out time for the simple walking that Jorgensen did when she first arrived in San Francisco. "You get so caught up in what's going on inside the building," Barsody said, "that you forget to pay attention to your feet."

The walking can be the openhearted wandering of a person on a street retreat, or it can be the more intentional "walking-with" that the Faithful Fools call accompaniment. **Alex Darr**, a lay outreach minister for the Faithful Fools, was the point person accompanying Bruce, who had lived on the streets for thirty-one years and panhandled on the corner near the First UU Church of San Francisco.

Darr grew up in the San Francisco church and had heard of the Faithful Fools. But he didn't have much faith that a Unitarian Universalist ministry would have a deep understanding of the Tenderloin, which Darr thought he knew, because he had friends among the artists and rock musicians who live in the neighborhood. Meanwhile, he had met Bruce Meyer, who at that time was panhandling in his neighborhood. Pointing at his long, red beard, Bruce would call Alex "the Amish guy" and regale him with tales of his life on the streets.

Then Darr did a street retreat—and another one, as a shadower of youth doing a street retreat as part of their congregation's Coming of Age program. "Within an hour I saw it was a very different way of being in the Tenderloin," Darr said. "Shadowing kids, and hearing their reflections on their experience—plus my own experience—really sold me on the process." At Leadership School for the Pacific Central District—Darr was a member of the Board of Trustees and an active leader in San Francisco—he learned the importance of listening with no agenda, without trying to "fix" anything.

So he began listening to Meyer's stories in a different way. One day, Darr was supposed to meet a friend at the Asian Art Museum, but Bruce was talking, and Alex was listening, and Darr couldn't tear himself away. "I kept listening until finally I could see something I could do that might be of help to Bruce," he said. "I told him I would go with him when he cashed his welfare check every month, and hold it for him—give him ten dollars a day, so he could get his fix and not have to panhandle from a place of desperation, where he was yelling at people on the corner."

Soon Meyer asked Darr if he could help him get off heroin and onto methadone, and that was when the real ride began. Darr spent more than a full day on the telephone, until he finally found a free program that would take Meyer. He went with Meyer to a hospital emergency room, where Meyer faked a chest injury so he could get the X-ray mandated for admission to the program. Meyer checked in—but stayed only through the weekend. "Too many rules," he said.

"Then he started talking about paying money for a detox program," Darr said, and the Fools thought that might be worth an investment. With financial support from the Faithful Fools, Meyer completed the twenty-one-day detox, stayed off dope another week or so, then lapsed back to heroin.

"Then he said, 'You know, I could maybe do this if I didn't have to stay on the street, if I was inside where I could lay down and watch TV.'" So the Fools decided to up the ante and help Bruce stay in a hotel room while his case for Social Security Disability Income—which he seemed sure to win eventually—made its way through the courts.

As this was beginning to unfold, Darr had decided to attend General Assembly in Long Beach and stay on the streets. Every day, Darr sat outside the convention center with a sign—hand-painted on cardboard—that said, "Will come to GA for change," and engaged GA attendees in conversation about what he was doing. It was then that he began to see his work with the Fools as ministry, but it wasn't until he missed an interview for a job at the Exploratorium science museum that he knew ministry was his vocation.

Darr missed the interview, because he was guarding the electric wheelchair of one of the street people who regularly panhandled outside the San Francisco church. "I had just washed Johnny's wheelchair for the second time," Darr said, "and I was waiting for him to get out of the hospital. And the time for my interview was approaching, and I was waiting, and I had to just let it go by. Because I realized that there were lots of people who could do that job at the Exploratorium, but I could not think of anybody else who could sit by that chair."

Darr stopped looking for full-time work, instead making ends meet with odd jobs and receiving financial support from the Faithful Fools when he couldn't make his rent any other way. He was thinking about how to formalize his ministry with the San Francisco church. For the moment, he had decided not to go to seminary.

Bruce Meyer said Darr's nonjudgmental listening is what helped him change his life. "He doesn't get in trouble; he doesn't fight, and he's helped me learn to use my words and not fight," Meyer said.

Now Bruce attends Faithful Fools events in a different capacity. At a Fourth of July street-side barbecue, he cooked for nearly one hundred people. It was his chance to reconnect with people he had known while he was living on the streets—to show them that change is possible, and to introduce them to his friends.

CHAPLAINS: COMMUNITIES OF CARE

One of the most familiar faces of community ministry is that of the chaplain, whose communities generally are built inside institutions that are not connected to Unitarian Universalism—hospitals, prisons, public and private agencies, and the US Armed Forces. Chaplains usually serve in interfaith settings in which evangelism is not appropriate, but their presence nevertheless links the UU movement to wider communities and extends the UU mission visibly outside the church walls and the parish bounds.

The Rev. **Cynthia Kane** took it to the United States Navy, and, as a commissioned Lieutenant, has served at Arlington National Cemetery, aboard the USS *John C. Stennis* (an aircraft carrier home ported in Washington state), and at Guantanamo Bay, Cuba, where the United States was detaining terrorism suspects.

On the *Stennis* her typical day would start at 4:00 a.m. with physical training, followed by morning muster, in which the people in her department got together to hear the Plan of the Day. Then, it was to her office, to meet the line of Sailors and Marines already forming up outside her door. They are "wonderful young adults from a different cultural, socioeconomic, and theological background than we find in most of our UU congregations," who come with a range of issues. "A morning counseling load might include one who just found out his girlfriend is pregnant; another who got drunk the night before and is about to answer for it at Captain's Mast; one who is being deployed to Iraq; one who doesn't know how to balance a budget."

Many of them have a notion of God that is the "old white, bearded guy in the clouds" or maybe Jesus; while God for Kane is not a physical being but an inner sense that accompanies her and carries her through. It has helped some of them to know that Kane herself is willing to argue with God—"What is it that you are doing here?" she might ask, shaking her fist at the sky—and call it prayer.

Military values are consistent, she maintains, with Unitarian Universalist values. "In the military, we take an oath to support, defend, and bear allegiance to the US Constitution. Well, the First Amendment is about freedom of religion. Ours is a faith with different understandings of God. My job is to continue to defend that."

Lt. Kane considers herself a pacifist, and as a noncombatant sees an opportunity to do the work of peace through understanding the ways of war. The Rev. **Tom Korson** is a chaplain in a very different environment—a program for homeless people in Denver—but he similarly has had to adapt his mission to fit the mission of his institution.

Korson is chaplain at Newgenesis, a transitional community for the homeless, a 130-bed, modified residential therapeutic community, which he described as a "structured program designed to help homeless people who are working or capable of working to move from the streets into independent housing."

Korson came into ministry from the world of law, and originally planned a community ministry in education, perhaps teaching courses in law and religion, combining his new knowledge with his life experience as a lawyer. An internship with an interfaith association led him to focus his learning on one of the group's ministries, and he began working one day a week at what was then called Central Shelter. His presence there grew to a half-time staff position as chaplain.

When he began the work, he acutely felt the gulf between the circumstances of the residents and his social location of privilege; he also felt the theological gap between his liberal Christianity and the fundamentalist, "sometimes triumphalist" Christianity of some of the residents. Moreover, he began his ministry there with "what the social and political conservatives referred to as a 'bleeding heart liberal' attitude. Influenced by our Principles and Purposes, I viewed homelessness from a systemic point of view."

But the agency he served looked at homelessness differently. In its own statements, it points out that it "does not view the homeless as members of a privileged class." It does not advocate at City Hall on behalf of the homeless as a group. Sometimes, Korson said, he wishes the agency would be more proactive on behalf of its residents. But Newgenesis remains true to its philosophy: the therapeutic community formed by the residents themselves is the primary force for healing.

The chaplain's role is to be a pastoral presence, helping the residents affirm their strengths. "In some situations," he said, "I help them on a pastoral level to deal with deep hurts that have prevented them from leading truly fulfilling lives." The residents seem to appreciate that he is a staff member but not an enforcer of rules. At the same time, he said, the residents know that Korson will not advocate for them if they are at loggerheads with a staff member. "They know that my role is to encourage them to move on with their lives," he said, "and not dwell excessively in the past."

His work at Newgenesis has led Korson to roles in the wider community as well. He serves on an interagency committee exploring ways to assist ex-offenders in reintegration into society once their prison terms are up. Sixty-five percent of the residents at Newgenesis are former prison inmates, Korson said, and he sees this involvement as another way to address the problems that trap them.

"All God's children deserve attention, respect and opportunities," Korson said. "The 'opportunities' part is what is consistent with what Newgenesis is offering. People of faith—everybody, really—should be aware of or involved in these issues."

The church that ordained him, First Unitarian of Denver, remains involved in the program, which it considers to be "a ministry beyond its walls." Once a month, the church provides a meal for men staying at the shelter. And several church members have visited the main facility to learn more about its operation. "The congregation values the fact that I am ministering to the marginalized," Korson said. "This is work that most congregants can't do."

෬෨

If community ministry occurs, as Rebecca Parker has said, in the "liminal spaces" where relations are eroded by mistrust and suffering, then the Rev. **Kate Bortner** has found an unexpected but auspicious location to build a community ministry—the police department of York, Pennsylvania.

Bortner has been for many years the Crime Prevention Coordinator for the York City Police Department, a staff position that includes working with volunteer police chaplains as well as providing direct pastoral care, preaching, social witness, advocacy, worship, and ritual. By her estimate, about half her job involves pastoral care—listening to citizens, police officers, and volunteer chaplains, making sure they know that they have been heard.

She calls it "a ministry of availability and introduction."

She observes at close hand the pain of police officers who enter law enforcement out of "deeply held faith, values, or commitment to service," and find themselves "reviled, mistrusted, and hated." The reality of life on the streets plus the expectations of "rigid, often repressive 'blue culture'" tend to erode identity, faith, relationship, and connection to family in the individual officer, producing "wounds so deep they are hardly ever spoken aloud."

In addition to being available as a listening ear, Bortner teaches about safety issues and the police role in community action—from formal classroom instruction to television and radio appearances. She works with the city's community policing program, schools, and initiatives for adults and youth.

And she works to build effective community partnerships between police and at least twenty community agencies, including the United Way, Domestic Violence Task Force, Interfaith Alliance, and York County Community Against Racism. Sometimes she is called on to design community rituals of healing such as a Victims Rights Vigil and March, a Homicide Survivors Memorial Service, and a 9/11-anniversary observance.

When she thinks of Parker's call for community ministry to "ask us to stay at the table when conflict threatens to send us to our separate, safer circles," Bortner thinks of the wounded areas where police are called first to restore safety, and ministers are called to rebuild trust. "Our mandate," she said, "is to tend to those tender areas before they erupt into bloody wounds that drain the life force from our communal body." She sees her role—and the police role—as helping to "build the peace instead of just keeping it."

Bortner's job in the Police Department and her role in the Unitarian Universalist congregation in York grew side by side. When she decided to go to seminary, it was because she was coming to see her job as ministry. As she proceeded through seminary, she involved police supervisors every step of the way—in her field education, in her seminary midpoint review, in her internship, and in independent studies.

Meanwhile her relationship with the York congregation continued to deepen, and eventually was formalized in a Covenant of Agreement that includes an annual job review, a Ministry Support Team, monthly attendance at staff meetings, and regular meetings with the parish minister. "Establishing effective working relationships both with the congregation and the police department through eight ministers—settled and interim—three mayors, and six police executive commanders is something I am very proud of," she said.

With the congregation, the community minister is in a position to "share stories of world and church." Bortner believes it is the community minister's role to keep the door open for that sharing.

৩৩

Whether in homelessness, facing fire in the military, in conflict situations involving law enforcement, or in hospitals, people who are struggling often need a pastor. This kind of ministry—pastoral ministry—gives the person in crisis "the gift of knowing he is not alone," in the words of the Rev. **Ben Hall** of Providence, Rhode Island. More than that, Hall said, "it gives the chaplain the privilege of seeing another person's woundedness not as an aberration but as a part of the truth of living. It's a chance to be reminded that we are all in this together, and to embrace this."

Hall is employed by The Chaplaincy Center, a nonprofit agency in Providence that provides pastoral care and Clinical Pastoral Education for people and institutions in Southern New England. One of the Center's contract agencies, the state-run Eleanor Slater Hospital, contracts with the Center to have Hall serve as its full-time director of pastoral care.

Hall tells this story of a chaplain's life in the hospital:
One time, at the beginning of Friday Worship, our weekly nondenominational Christian service in the Adult

Psychiatric Services building, a patient calls out excitedly, "Can I do a reading today?"

"Sure!" I tell him. He quickly follows up: "Can I do a sermon today?" I tell him, "Not today," but say he and I can meet next week to prepare a sermon for him to teach sometime in the future. A little while later, after he has read the reading from the Letter to the Philippians, and after I've offered a few words about what I hear in this reading, I invite the patients to share their reflections. The same patient's hand goes up like lightning.

He tells how when he's walking outside and feels a warm feeling in his chest, he knows that it's Jesus, and it makes him remember how God is always with him, and how God is always with all of us. Then this same patient offers more: he tells how, in a dream he once had, "God high-fived me."

We laugh with him, all of us at once aware of the comedy of the image and its deep truth. I ask him, "When God high-fived you, what was God telling you? What was that another way of saying?"

Without too much of a pause, he answers, "I think he was saying, 'You're doing all right kid. Keep it up! I'm with ya all the way.'"

After the beauty of his words have a chance to sink in, to touch each of our hearts, I have a realization, and I tell the patient, "Remember how you wanted to teach a sermon today? Well, you just did."

Hall is in covenant as community minister with the Religious Society of Bell Street Chapel in Providence. As their community minister, Hall preaches once or twice a year, attends worship and other events regularly, serves on the Parish and Social Concerns Committee, provides emergency pastoral care occasionally when the parish minister is away, and "seeks to be in frequent and fruitful dialogue with the parishioners about the ways in which my ministry in the hospital and with CPE students can be a vital ministry of the congregation itself." He tries to bring the fruits of what he's learning in the world beyond the parish bounds back to the congregation, as much as he brings what he learns in his church community to his work in the wider world.

BUILDING COMMUNITY
THROUGH ADMINISTRATION

The most visible public face Unitarian Universalism presents to the world is the face of a community minister. Like all the ministers who serve the association at 25 Beacon Street in Boston, and in district offices around the nation, the Rev. **Bill Sinkford** is a community minister. But unlike many, the seventh president of the Unitarian Universalist Association was fellowshipped from the start as a community minister.

That was not his plan, however, when he entered seminary.

Sinkford had spent years holding management positions in marketing with major corporations and had run his own business, Sinkford Restorations, Inc. He heard his call to ministry in a simple question put to him by the Rev. Marilyn Sewell, then minister of his home congregation in Cincinnati.

"I was in a period of my life where I knew I needed to make a change," Sinkford said. "I was in the construction business, and my body would not allow me to do that indefinitely."

"At the same time I had become very involved in my home church, doing all the things good lay folks do. The church had become a more important part of my life." Then, at an NAACP dinner, Sewell turned to him and popped her question: "Have you ever considered ministry?"

"I knew right then that that was what I was called to do," Sinkford said.

He assumed, then, that it was a call to *parish* ministry. But while he was still in seminary at Starr King School for the Ministry, his wife became sick, and he needed to find work.

"It was one of those acts of grace that John Buehrens, then president of the Association and my former college roommate, was looking for someone to fill the district services job at the UUA."

His job in Boston became his community ministry internship, and he was fellowshipped in the community ministry track. As he worked in UUA administration, he began to hear a different call.

"I came to see that I was in some ways almost uniquely suited to institutional leadership, given my business background, ability to manage large structures, and a pastoral calling—which is in religious community an essential part of institutional leadership."

What surprised him was that being president of the UUA calls on so many of the traditional skills of ministry—a prophetic role in the public square, a significant pastoral role as minister at large to Unitarian Universalism, a teaching role sharing information, "and I get to preach actually a little more often than I would like"—sixty or seventy times in a year, though he was quick to point out that he gets to use the same sermon more than once.

Sinkford's election made history in the Association, as the first African-American elected to the office. As president of the Unitarian Universalist Association, Sinkford serves as chief executive officer of the Association of a thousand-plus congregations, shaping its future alongside the Board of Trustees, responding to public events that call for religious witness, and pastoring the flock in large gatherings, such as the annual General Assembly, and smaller meetings throughout the year.

What was most satisfying to Sinkford in his first four-year term in office was his work in the public square.

The body of community ministers has a role in that, Sinkford believes. "Every time one of our ministers serves as a chaplain in a hospital or hospice, or increasingly in the military, we're offering Unitarian Universalism to people who are in need. And community ministries that are justice-making ministries have a very important part to play in our being that credible voice for liberal religious values. They are the ones that make that manifest."

COMMUNITY BUILDING AS JUSTICE MAKING IN THE PUBLIC SQUARE

The Rev. **Debra Haffner** had what she calls a "Road to Damascus" experience in 1975. She was serving as an intern in the US Congress, on her way to law school the next year ("having always been told that's what smart women did"), when she took a weeklong course in sexuality education. She had been raised in a home that was open about sexuality issues. In college she had become involved in the women's health movement, and had learned how many women had had oppressive and repressive experiences around sexuality. In one flash in 1975, she realized that she was called to help heal that brokenness.

"I marvel at the clarity I had then," she said. She withdrew her plans for law school and began work that would lead her eventually to the presidency of SIECUS—the Sexuality Information and Education Council of the United States. "When you're twenty, and you don't have a mortgage and a family, it's easier to listen to your heart."

The next time she had such an experience, she didn't listen quite so readily.

It was 1989. She was giving a talk on sexuality and religion in her Unitarian Universalist congregation, and she felt a voice telling her, "This is the work you're supposed to do"—to turn her vocation more explicitly into a ministry. "My Jewish, Unitarian background didn't allow for such voices," she said, "so I ignored it."

But the call persisted. So in 1996 she took a sabbatical as president of SIECUS to try out seminary. In 2000, she resigned her position at SIECUS, even though she knew such a move meant a substantial loss of income and—it seemed—the loss of a national platform for her views and her voice. "I did it," she said, "not knowing whether the ministry I had envisioned—combining sexuality and ministry—was anything anyone would want."

It turned out that people did want it—and need it. The issues of clergy sexual abuse, ordination of clergy who are members of sexual minorities, and marriage equality were bubbling as Haffner completed seminary and entered preliminary fellowship. What has surprised her most is the great silence on issues of sexuality by most religious organizations.

"Most clergy receive no training on sexuality issues," she said. "The point of a lot of my writing is that most congregations have ignored the issues of sexuality that people come to us with, whether it's a history of violent abuse, difficulties in couple relationships, questions about gender identity and sexual orientation, issues about how to provide sexuality education to children, and so on."

Becoming a minister deepened her understanding of God, of the importance of a faith community in people's lives, and of what it means to be a UU minister. "What hasn't changed is my theology, which has always been incarnational. I have always believed that the closest we come to the divine is in our interactions with each other. And there is nothing more important than how we treat each other."

Haffner did a parish internship that included a community component—continuing to develop the Religious Declaration on Sexual Morality, Justice, and Healing, which Haffner had begun as president of SIECUS. By September 2005 the declaration—which endorses a right to sexual lives that "express love, justice, mutuality, commitment, consent, and pleasure"—had been endorsed by more than 2,400 religious leaders.

The Declaration is available on the website of the Religious Institute on Sexual Morality, Justice, and Healing, which Haffner co-founded with the Rev. Larry Greenfield.

In 2003, the Unitarian Universalist Association asked Haffner to develop a manual on how to welcome a person with a history of sex offenses into UU congregations while keeping children, youth, and vulnerable adults safe from abuse and exploitation. The handbook was published online in 2005 as "Balancing Acts: Keeping Children Safe in Congregations." With the UUA's permission, Haffner has adapted it for Christian and Jewish congregations, and it is available in print from the Christian Community and LifeQuest.

Haffner, an experienced and successful fundraiser with SIECUS, has found fund-raising for the Institute tougher going, and sees this as an issue for the wider community ministry movement. And, having just turned fifty, she was increasingly aware of the "need to be mentoring younger people to do what I do." One way to do this is to supervise interns, which Haffner intended to begin once she completed final fellowship.

Her work is to "promote a progressive religious voice on sexuality in the public square." In doing so, she feels blessedly supported by the UU tradition of leadership on issues of healthy sexuality. "The UUA has been a beacon on sexual issues that no other denomination has," Haffner said.

࿚

When she decided it was time to leave the parish, the Rev. **Lindi Ramsden** didn't know she was heading for community ministry. After eighteen successful years as minister of the First Unitarian Church of San Jose, she was ready for new challenges but didn't yet know what they would be.

Ramsden and her congregation had built a strong community presence from the parish. "I don't see a huge separation between ministry to the people in a congregation and ministry to the larger community of which we are a part," she said. "We all walk out of the doors on Sunday; everyone is affected by what is going on in that larger community."

Ramsden began studying economic policy and California history, out of her own deepening interest in forces that shape the community landscape. She had noticed in her congregation that people, whether Silicon Valley managers or those who were barely making it, had similar issues: "People have no time—whether it is because they're not making a living wage or because they're working for a company that is downsizing, stretching its corporate leadership to the max."

"Globalization had erased all the protections that were there," Ramsden said. "It reminded me a lot of the 1880s, when capitalism got out ahead of all the agreements on how to safeguard human life."

"You can't separate the impact of the community on people's spiritual life and development."

Not yet knowing what her next ministry would be, she agreed on a contract basis to do an implementation plan for the newly developing UU Legislative Ministries of California. She saw an opportunity to create a ministry that would "strengthen social justice networks among UUs, so we can better empower our principles in the public square."

As the organization's executive director, Ramsden travels the state, building support for UULM-California and urging social action committees to begin with a "listening campaign" to learn what really matters to members of the congregation. "We're trying to bring a different flavor to social justice work so it really is a ministry," she said, "so it includes worship, friendships—the things that fill us up and sustain us."

"I don't know who originally said that Unitarian Universalism is a religion with a spiritual center and a civic circumference, but I use it a lot," she said. "If you're only out in the civic arena and you've forgotten to nurture that center—that interest in the wholeness of life—it's easy to feel discouraged or bitter, or that the responsibility to change the whole world is resting on your shoulders."

Marriage equality is one of three focus issues selected by the UULM after soliciting questionnaires from UUs up and down the state. Health care—an issue on which Ramsden said there is great potential for alliances and partnerships—was another. And the third issue, water rights—or, as Ramsden prefers to call it, "water democracy"— was chosen as an "incubator issue," one that is likely to grow in importance as more communities are pressured to privatize their water systems and water supplies.

"In any one of our congregations there are people with amazing knowledge and access to power in their communities on a variety of issues, as well as people who may be deeply and personally affected by some issue," she said. "They could do amazing work as UUs if there's space for them to do it."

Encouraging congregation-based social justice ministries, Ramsden urges congregations to consider hiring community ministers to pastor the work from the parish. She points to "the kind of dramatic change that happens in congregations when we bring in professionals to do a part of the work, or even when we hire a part-time Director of Religious Education in what had been an all-volunteer RE program.

"How do we empower our principles?" she said. "You look at the Purposes and Principles, and they're very justice-oriented, but we haven't invested very much financially in helping staff deepen and develop those ministries."

She would like to see more social justice ministers hired by large congregations. She encourages smaller churches to think about cooperating in hiring a social justice minister to serve several congregations. And she continues to believe that parish ministers have a strong community role. "I want to say that parish ministry, if you do it right, *is* community ministry."

꿍

COMMUNITY BUILDING IN THE ACADEMY: MINISTRIES OF EDUCATION

A community of empowerment emerges when congregations unite around a shared purpose, such as protecting the Earth by saving energy or building capacity for justice-making in a district. It can also happen in a classroom.

At Hastings College in Hastings, Nebraska, the Rev. Dr. **M. Jean Heriot** works to empower students to discover their vocation through community reflection on their work in the world for justice.

Finding her own call to teaching and to ministry was no straight line. Heriot came from a whole family of educators. "When I went to graduate school the one thing I was determined not to be was a teacher," Heriot said. But on her way to a doctorate in cultural anthropology, she was offered a teaching assistantship, and she took it. "And I found that I loved teaching."

Her particular passion was the study of religion. She grew up in the rural South, and had found herself sitting in church at an early age asking hard questions. "Why did the church ministers preach one thing—for example, 'justice for all'—and then not live that promise?" she had wondered.

Heriot had started looking for answers in social work, then shifted to cultural anthropology. "I kept asking myself questions about lived religion—that is, what do the people themselves have to say about religion, life, ritual, and their own theologies of life?" She began looking for a church, and she found Unitarian Universalism.

Five years later she enrolled at the Pacific School of Religion. She still loved teaching, but there was something missing. "I felt the spiritual or religious dimension of life wasn't being brought into the classroom," she said. "I wanted to find a way to teach and write and be part of that conversation."

She took a teaching job to keep the debt load down while she was in seminary. Hired to teach religious studies at a Jesuit university, Heriot said, "I could bring faith into the classroom. I didn't have to stick to a social science perspective.

"Students were integrating their own faith struggles in the class-room," she said. "They might be studying violence, and having conflict in their own faith community, so they would ask, 'What does it mean that my church has conflict in it?' Or if they were studying death in a particular culture, they would ask, 'What does that mean?' to their own understanding."

Ordained by her home congregation in Palo Alto, she shifted her fellowship track to community ministry.

Ultimately, her drive to encourage people to find and pursue their own passion for justice led her to the Vocation and Values Program at Hastings, where she is associate director of vocational discernment and service learning. She calls the position "the most harmonious blending of ministry, education, and social justice I have yet to experience." Although the nearest UU congregation is more than one hundred miles from the college, Heriot is affiliated as a community minister with Lincoln Unitarian Church.

At Hastings she teaches service learning classes and promotes service learning to other faculty. Heriot said "service learning" is part of a movement to encourage students to be deeply engaged with the world through experiential learning. Generally, it involves meaningful service in a nonprofit agency that meets identified community needs and is tied to a classroom learning environment.

In community, the students learn—from listening to themselves and one another—what it means to live the prophetic injunction to "do justice, love mercy, and walk humbly" with God, Heriot said. The justice work they are doing out in the world "calls into question the materialism of their own lives, what goals they have, how are they going to live them."

Heriot's guides are religious educators such as Parker Palmer and Sophia Fahs, who "work to engage students and adults in the deep and thought-provoking questions that will never go away"; and activists who have worked for justice throughout the world—the Rev. Martin Luther King Jr., Mohandas Gandhi, Rosa Parks, Saul Alinsky,

Paul Rogat Loeb, Starhawk—as well as the Unitarian Universalist movement itself.

This work feeds her soul and keeps her committed to justice. "As I reflect on community ministry, one area of our service to the world is this prophetic work," she said. "Justice calls to us and asks, 'How will you make this world new again? How will you live your faith? What, oh what, are you called to do?'"

ᡣᡅ

The Rev. **Cheryl Leshay** remembers her own college experience as a time of a crisis of faith. She left her home in Oklahoma and her fundamentalist Baptist church community to travel east and plunge into a world of religious choices at Smith College in Northampton, Massachusetts. "I had come from a family that had lots of clergy and missionary stuff in its history," she said, "so I was predisposed to have a spiritual crisis."

In the searching that ensued, Leshay became in succession a Reform Jew, a student of Buddhism, and a feminist witch. She met two Unitarian Universalists, but she didn't know they were UUs, or even what UUs were. "I had no chaplain," she said. "I had no place to take this except my classes."

Now, many years later, she is "a UU completely. And I know that if I had had someone…there for me at that critical time, I would have gotten here a lot easier."

With twelve institutions of higher education in Worcester, Massachusetts, where she resides, Leshay has begun to build a ministry of community building, supporting liberal religious clubs on several of the campuses.

Leshay felt her first call to a ministry of religious education as a teacher in her daughter's RE program. Soon she was employed as a part-time director of religious education, and she realized, "I had found something I wanted to do not just as a part-time job. This was my calling in life—to connect people to their faith." She went to seminary, "healing myself along the way," and worked at many UU congregations and as RE consultant in the Ballou-Channing District.

The work was good, but Leshay hungered for the kind of holy connection she had felt as a hospital chaplain during her Clinical Pastoral Education training. There, she said, "I had a chance to work in an ecumenical kind of way. I got to be chaplain to people who worshipped in Spanish in a storefront church: to a Catholic woman who was praying her husband would die because she couldn't figure out how to get out of the marriage and he was abusing her; to a surgeon who was afraid his patient would die on the operating table. It wasn't me; it was the role. God was doing the work."

Eventually, she needed to find a ministry in her hometown. She had accompanied her daughter to college interviews and had heard her ask every recruiter: "Do you have a campus ministry?"

"I was paying attention, listening to my daughter," Leshay said. Her daughter enrolled at Worcester Polytechnic Institute, where she met a student who was trying to start a liberal religious group. Leshay had already been in conversation with the Rev. Ralph Galen, who had been supporting this campus group, and who was looking for a way to hand it off.

"When I started listening to the students, I had that same feeling as when I had been a hospital chaplain," Leshay said. "I had the feeling that what I needed would show up for me." The conviction was growing in her that this was a call. "We have twelve institutions of higher education in Worcester," she said, "and there are no liberal chaplaincies among them except Hillel at Clark University." Meanwhile, the Christian right is on every campus. "This is unacceptable," Leshay said. "You never do more sorting out of yourself until the first time you leave home. This is when it happens in people's lives. We don't have a right not to be there."

There are few resources for campus ministry in the UU movement. "If you look at how people plan on funding campus ministry, it's through the $600 you might make once a year in a worship service you might or might not have," Leshay said. "Or, the expectation is that one of the big congregations will feed a part-time staff minister to do campus ministry. We don't have that in Worcester. But we do have twelve institutions."

Leshay put together a committee of college professors and UU ministers to brainstorm ways to make it work. With their guidance, she began to support student-run clubs. She pursued a number of potential funding sources, exploring district sponsorship and sending mail to students coming to these campuses as UUs, to their congregations, and to UU alumni of the Worcester colleges, as well as seeking support from UU churches in the district. She also reached out to other liberal religious organizations with greater resources, such as the American Baptists and the United Church of Christ. She or members of her committee—always in the company of a student—preached about the program in area churches on Sundays.

She is affiliated as a community minister with the UU Church of Worcester on Holden Street, which supports her ministry by acting as her fiscal agent and giving her space to work. The church also has plans to host a regional campus ministry conference.

Although it is the chaplaincy that she loves, a lot of what she is doing is administrative—helping the student groups figure out how to negotiate their own campus bureaucracies and become a presence on campus. "I'm trying to put this organization together so it will survive me," she said. "Its goal is to make sure these groups on campus will survive as students leave every four years. If we don't train leaders on campus, they're going to be gone when the kid who started the group is finished."

"These are the kids who are going to be in charge in another ten years," Leshay said. "I don't want their only religious resource to be fundamentalism."

〜

JUSTICE AND CARING: BEACON HOUSE COMMUNITY MINISTRY WASHINGTON, DC

The Rev. **Donald E. Robinson** has a vision that Beacon House, which offers tutoring, college prep programs, and other services to the underprivileged children of a housing project in northeast District of Columbia, could grow to serve one thousand children and youth each day.

119

From 1965 to 1986, Robinson worked as a social worker—in the school system, in youth correctional facilities, and in community agencies—and over those nineteen years, he felt driven to find a way to help the youth he was encountering. Because, he said, these youth "weren't going to make it unless they had somebody in their corner."

"You'd have to understand, they had no control over it," he said. "By the time they were six or seven, they'd been molded in the wrong way."

"Oh Lord, it angered me, because I thought the conditions were systemic. They could have been improved if society wanted to improve them. It angered me greatly. I know and I knew then, those conditions did not have to exist."

Robinson wanted to create a program that would minister to the whole person—physical, social, and spiritual. He knew he needed to prepare himself.

And he knew he needed help. "You can't do it alone. I needed some connections; I needed lots of people." He enrolled at Howard University Divinity School.

He had found his own spiritual community at All Souls Unitarian Universalist Church in Washington, where he had been drawn to by the strong social justice program. He was drawn there, too, by the many different kinds of people at All Souls. "I thought, to me that's what it's about. If you're going to be spiritual, if you're going to serve the life force, you can't segregate yourself."

Robinson was ordained at All Souls in 1990 and went off in search of a community to build his vision. He looked at Edgewood Terrace, where the Tenant Association president, Rogerline Nicholson, listened to his dream and joined him in a partnership to transform the community.

Next Robinson met with members of several of the UU churches from around the Beltway, and it was out of these meetings that the name Beacon House Community Ministry emerged.

When Beacon House started out, it was located in a vacant, four-bedroom apartment. Robinson survived on a small retirement check from his years in social work, and filled in working for caterers on the weekends to make enough to get by.

It all got a lot easier when Bob Johnsen, a member of the River Road UU Church in Bethesda, Maryland, and a professional community organizer, showed up to help. Eventually the program moved to a six-thousand-square-foot community center in Edgewood Terrace.

In the early days, it was Robinson alone, helping as many children as he could with their homework. Now the program employs an executive director, an education director, an athletic director, and a development officer. Robinson spends much of the day planning and promoting the program around the city and the nation.

He still sits with the children whenever he can, helping with homework or pitching baseballs. He buys things for the children out of his own pocket. "People want to know why I do that, " he said. "I tell them, 'Well, that's my child. When people have children, that's what they do.'"

Many of the young people with whom the program worked in the early years are in college or vocational programs. And, Robinson says, "I think they'll be much better parents than their parents have been to them."

For Robinson, part of the joy of Beacon House has been "bringing the city and the suburbs together, white and black." The Beltway UU church members are among the corps of tutors and mentors who spend time one-on-one with the children of Edgewood Terrace.

"We're breaking down the barriers between white and black, and it will last forever," Robinson said. "They look at each other differently. The people from the suburbs, they understand now that these kids aren't all bad. And the people in the city, they see all these white folks coming in from the suburbs and they say, damn, these are good folks too."

"It just keeps me going to see the world as a better place, where all ethnic groups can befriend one another. Help one another."

The biggest challenge remains resources: volunteers and money. "Volunteers are always a struggle, especially getting volunteers of color. We do have some, but we just don't get enough to come in and volunteer in this program."

"And money. If I had more money, I could do a lot of things. Save a lot more children."

121

CARING FOR THE WHOLE PERSON

For the Rev. **Barbara Meyers**, the theological journey began where most ministers visit only as a chaplain—in a locked ward of a mental hospital.

Meyers was a high-functioning, PhD-holding computer scientist. She loved her job and her life, but after she gave birth to her daughter, postpartum depression struck so severely that she was in danger of taking her own life. She was taken to a psychiatric hospital.

With medication and therapy, she quickly got back on her feet, and was released after two weeks. But she was shaken. She had not liked being around "those kinds of people": people who were schizophrenic—people who needed to be locked up. They were defective human beings, she thought, and now she was a defective human being too. She had a mental illness.

Several years later she sought the help of a therapist for her persistent feelings of shame and unhappiness. The therapy was effective, and Meyers began to feel happy—spontaneously happy—for the first time in a long time. "I don't know where this came from," she told her psychiatrist, and he answered, "It came from you."

"This was the first time I ever got the concept that God could be inside," Meyers said. She got so happy, she stopped taking her medication, and wound up in the same locked ward where she had been a patient eight years earlier—but this time it was different. "I saw that these were not defective human beings, but they were children of God," she said. "That's where I got my first idea of Universalism: that all people are God's children, and God loved them, and God loved me."

When she was released she went looking for a religious community, and found the Unitarian Universalists.

She got deeply involved in her church community, and became a founding member of a new church in Fremont, California. As a member of the Worship Committee, she and a group of others were planning a service on "spiritual autobiography," and Meyers delivered a homily about her experiences with mental illness and therapy. Her homily received so much positive interest in the community that

Meyers was moved to convene and run a depression support group at the church.

As the group grew, Meyers said, she began to think she ought to have some training in pastoral counseling, so she enrolled as a special student in a course at Starr King School for the Ministry. It was in this course that she began to wonder whether she might have a call to professional ministry.

Completing her retirement eligibility at IBM, she enrolled full-time at Starr King at the age of fifty-three.

She did a community/parish hybrid internship at the Faithful Fools Street Ministry and the First Unitarian Universalist Society of San Francisco. At the church she started a depression support group and a grief support group, each of which included people from both the congregation and the street community of the Faithful Fools.

She was ordained on her fifty-eighth birthday and endorsed as a community minister by her home church, Mission Peak Unitarian Universalist of Fremont, California. Part of her ministry is to serve the church by heading the team of Pastoral Associates, and by providing pastoral care and an occasional sermon when the minister is away. She has written a curriculum to educate congregations on how to be intentionally supportive of people with mental illness and their families; from this came *The Caring Congregation Handbook*, published by Will To Print Press, a program of the Faithful Fools.

Meyers is supported by her pension, she is paid by the Fremont church for the pastoral work she does there, and she also has a small paying job as an assistant director of Life Reaching Across to Life, a peer support group for people with mental problems.

"I've had so many blessings—home, family, a supportive husband, insurance, a wonderful doctor, a kind of mental health issue that is easily stabilized with medication," she said. "Some of the people I've worked with don't have any of those advantages, and yet they still wake up each day with a lot of courage in a system that basically kicks them around. They're my heroes."

∽

Whether healing takes place in a community or individual therapeutic setting, the pastoral care work that ministers do often connects to issues of mental health, and many ministers have found vocations in spiritual direction or life coaching—modalities that help people move toward greater integration in their lives, including psychotherapy.

The Rev. Dr. **Flo Gelo** currently serves the fellowship at Collegeville, Pennsylvania as a full-time called minister. In her journey toward called parish ministry, however, she found her experience with community ministries invaluable.

Gelo was working as a psychologist assistant in a forensic unit of an inpatient psychiatric center before she decided to go to seminary. She enrolled at Andover Newton Theological School, planning to study pastoral psychotherapy. But while she was working as director of religious education at First Parish Church at Needham, Massachusetts, the Rev. John Baker encouraged her to think of herself as a parish minister as well as a community minister.

For a time she was co-director of Ministry to the Homeless at Roxbury, Massachusetts, where she offered companionship to people living on the streets of Boston, conducted worship services at shelters, and visited many homeless men and women in hospitals.

She took a job as an interfaith, multicultural campus minister at the University of Pennsylvania, working for the Christian Association. Her primary responsibility was to supervise a lesbian-gay hotline as well as to develop programs in liberation and feminist theology. "Ministry on that urban campus was challenging and compelling," she said, "allowing me to address issues of sexism, racism, homophobia and peace and justice at all levels—interpersonal, institutional, and global."

Her experience with counseling students led to interest in psychotherapy that was "wholistic, blending the clinical and the spiritual." She began a training program in pastoral counseling and took a part-time position as a hospital chaplain, then moved to hospice and began teaching at a medical school, developing a curriculum in spirituality and medicine.

Her interest deepened into a specialization in grief and loss, and she entered a doctoral program and eventually sought credentialing from the American Association of Pastoral Counselors.

She began a private practice in psychotherapy, renting office space from a UU church, but each time a new minister came to the congregation, Gelo said, she had to renegotiate the relationship. She offered pastoral skills to the congregation, establishing a pastoral care program, assisting with difficult congregants, teaching and preaching, but these found "mixed support," so she moved her practice into a home office.

Through all these community ministries, Gelo found it both inspiring and helpful to be a UU in an interfaith setting. "Our principles of acceptance and affirmation of diversity, the primacy that we give to an authentic search for truth, and our insistence upon justice for all has become the source of inspiration and the core of my identity in ministry," she said.

৹

NEW COMMUNITIES RISING

Connie Yost started seminary to be a chaplain or a spiritual director. But her commitment in social justice would not leave her alone, and neither would her business background.

She was taking a course in community economic development at Claremont Theological School and working in low-income communities, where she was studying issues of poverty. At the same time, she had an assignment in another course to write a business plan for a nonprofit project. Yost had owned an employment agency, so a business plan was in no way daunting. But what would be her project?

At a conference on poverty and hunger, she heard a presentation by a young man who was involved in an urban farm-training program in Boston, The Food Project. He had started in this project at age fourteen. Now, at age twenty-two, he was taking what he had learned in that program and was running his own for-profit company making salsa out of the farm's fresh vegetables.

"It sounded so wonderful to me," Yost said. "Kids could be employed growing fruits and vegetables! Kids could make things, and learn. A lot clicked in my mind when I put it all together."

Yost is a Master Gardener, certified by the University of California Cooperative Extension. She began visiting entrepreneurial garden projects—one at the San Francisco County Jail and the Homeless Garden Project[149] in Santa Cruz—talking to people about how it works. Her dream was coming into focus: to create a Community Supported Agriculture garden and tie it in with schools, creating opportunities for youth to learn both gardening and management skills; and to sell shares of healthy, organic produce in a low-income community where healthy food choices are scarce.

But land, anywhere in or around Los Angeles, was expensive.

She visited the city manager, who was "not too enthusiastic." She opened talks with a memorial park. And she started building partnerships—with the Los Angeles Community Garden Council, and with local Unitarian Universalist churches.

Finally, she called the Los Angeles County Parks and Recreation Department's Whittier Narrows Park office, and officials there said they had an unused four-acre plot in the South El Monte neighborhood, just the kind of low-income neighborhood Yost was hoping to reach. LA County Supervisor Gloria Molina and the Parks and Recreation people were enthusiastic about the project—they gave the project a permit until 2008, did the initial plowing, and installed water to the site.

EarthWorks Enterprises was born.

"It was all a big learning," Yost said. "How long things take, how you have to keep working at it, over and over. I brought in community activists, well-known people who could push things through when they begin to bog down. The LA County Supervisors gave us seed money—a $25,000 grant. It's a long process."

Meanwhile, Yost petitioned the Ministerial Fellowship Committee to allow her to make this project her community ministry internship, supervised by the parish minister at Neighborhood Church in Pasadena. Part of the focus was to involve area churches in the

---

149 The Homeless Garden Project provides job training, transitional employment and support services to people who are homeless.

project. She went around and talked it up, and preached, and signed people up on an e-mail list, and collected some contributions.

"Without any district-wide projects like this," Yost said, "I didn't have any models. But having worked in a parish as part of my seminary training, I really wanted to do an internship relevant to my ministry."

That there were no churches close by the project presented a challenge. The closest church, Whittier, is tiny, but Yost is pleased that about three-quarters of the members got involved. And the project stirred some interest in the larger, suburban churches in Pasadena, Fullerton, Long Beach, and Orange Coast.

A hired manager and volunteers prepared the ground at the garden for its first planting; in September 2005 the first student workers from the South El Monte High School, which is within walking distance from the garden, arrived at the site. Yost also involved the Master Gardeners, who get community service credit toward renewing certification for helping the project. "After only a year we raised over $111,000," she said. "We have two and a half staff people, a nine-person board, and all these partnerships."

Yost sees Earth Works as a way to honor the UU Seventh Principle, as well as a way to affirm the inherent worth and dignity of all, especially youth. "We're showing a basic way for people to live in community and honoring that. We're supporting kids. We're growing food to support the health of the community and ourselves, being a place where we can come together as a community across all sorts of barriers—bringing people together who wouldn't necessarily have another reason to be together."

༄

The Rev. **Maddie Sifantus** starts her day with e-mail at 6:00 a.m. Golden Tones, the elder chorus she founded and has pastored since 1987, generates only half the volume in her in-box. Through her work with the chorus and the study to which that work led her, Sifantus has become an expert on end-of-life issues, and she is in demand as a speaker and consultant.

Golden Tones began when Sifantus, a professional singer, was asked to lead a little group of singers who had been meeting around a piano in a senior center. Now there are sixty members, who sing more than fifty concerts a year.

As she began working with what soon became the Golden Tones, Sifantus was studying the theology of Henry Nelson Weiman. His philosophy of God as a creative force that works with and within people and communities perfectly matched what began to happen with the Golden Tones.

"The group began to be a support for each other and an inspiration for frail elders. Here we were, bringing our gifts to the world's need, and doing it from a place of faith, and incredible things were happening."

"Anything I did to further the group's musicianship, or its camaraderie--or to deal with what was difficult--would be given back tenfold."

In this work her faith has grown into a recognition that God or the Holy is present all around, working through people.

After eighteen years, Sifantus worked to professionalize the operation, hiring an assistant director, and taking on a community ministry intern.

"I'm paid a salary, but I have no benefits," she said. "I'm in my mid-fifties, looking at how I'm going to support myself. It's a struggle to figure out how to make ends meet. But whenever I get discouraged about it, I go to a Golden Tones concert and see what's happening."

The Golden Tones performs at churches and community groups. Sifantus carries her music around in a tattered UU Service Committee bag, and sometimes people ask her about it. "I don't proselytize. Still, I consider this a way of doing mission and outreach for our faith. And I love that part of it."

She is affiliated as community minister with First Parish in Wayland, Massachusetts. She preaches once a year; she meets once a month with ministers of the church. She would like the relationship to be deeper. But as she discussed provisions for her new intern with the Intern Committee, she was pleased to hear one of the members say, "Golden Tones is one of the ministries of this church."

EXPANDING THE PARISH BOUNDS

Ministries often begin when an individual's "deep gladness"[150]—created by personal history, confirmed in life events or by a lucky confluence of interests with events—meets the world's deep need. Deep calls to deep, so it should be no surprise that many community ministries are born inside the parish. It is in working within the Unitarian Universalist tradition—noticing growth, celebrating depth—that one may first be inspired to call the community work one is doing "ministry."

Jim Cavenaugh's ministry developed from his work as a congregational lay leader. He was looking for an anti-racist, social justice project to propose for his congregation's first "all-church social action" initiative. A goal-setting process in the Unitarian Church of Harrisburg (Pennsylvania) had resulted in the intention to revitalize the church's social action presence in the community with a project that could involve the entire congregation.

"How about women in prison?" a friend advised. "They're underserved."

This opened up the possibility to do something both antiracist and pro-feminist, and Cavenaugh and others began to investigate possibilities. Wanting not to reinvent the wheel, they formed a partnership with a nonprofit already working in the area—The Program for Female Offenders.

The county jail was just a few miles from the church. The team did an in-reach into the congregation and an outreach into the community. They sponsored a play about women in prison. They bought books and held discussions. Then they began to move in simple, and not-so-simple, ways to be of service.

A simple way was for members of the congregation to bring the classified section of the Sunday paper to church, so they could be distributed to women seeking to re-enter society and find work.

Then they set up a clothing bank so re-entering women would have professional-looking clothes to wear for job interviews.

---

150 Frederick Buechner: "Where our deep gladness and the world's deep hunger meet, we hear a further call."

129

And they began a monthly training in paperwork management for the re-entering women. "Now a woman in this program might get a job interview from the want ads we brought in, schedule it in her day-minder that she got in the training we provided, and go to the interview in an outfit from a clothing donation from a member of our congregation," Cavenaugh said.

Along the way, Cavenaugh's friend, the Rev. Kate Bortner, told him he was doing community ministry. He enrolled in a course she took in UU history and polity at nearby Lancaster Theological Seminary. The next year he enrolled as a fulltime student. "I've always wanted to do something about the ills of this wounded world," Cavenaugh said.

Ultimately, he decided not to pursue ordination, which would have meant breaking or profoundly changing his relationship with his congregation and with its women in prison project. Instead he let seminary lead him more deeply into the work. He served one day a week as a volunteer chaplain in a county prison and volunteered with a local coalition of groups helping former inmates re-enter society. And he continued as a leader of a greatly expanded project in his congregation. Jim discovered that while his community ministry could have been expanded in some ways as an ordained ministry, the work he felt called to do did not require it, and by choosing to minister as a lay person, he had access to relationships that would not have been available to him otherwise.

We can see through Jim Cavenaugh's story that the decision to seek ordination as a community minister is one that opens some doors and closes others. It is a decision to be made thoughtfully and carefully, in the context of community.

∾

Just as there are lay and ordained ministers who take UU values and spirituality out into the community, there are ministers in parishes who bring community consciousness into the church and congregation. After Hurricane Katrina, parish ministers **Nina Grey** of First Unitarian in Chicago led a delegation of her congregation to New Orleans to help with the rebuilding, and **Phyllis O'Connell** of First Parish in Wellesley Hills, Massachusetts helped her congregation take on the year-long commitment to pay the mortgage of a hurricane ravaged congregation. **Sheldon Bennett**, parish minister at United First Parish in Quincy, Massachusetts, and **Anita Farber-Robertson,** when she was parish minister at the Unitarian Universalist Church of Greater Lynn, Massachusetts, were both active in bringing faith-based community organizing for social change (Industrial Area Foundation) into the greater Boston and greater Lynn communities, respectively. These organizations effect social change, not only by wisely wielding political power but also by weaving networks of mutuality between the different religious and ethnic faith communities. The congregations, thus involved themselves, become changed.

Parish minister **Steve Schick** helped his congregation in Haverhill, Massachusetts set up a soup kitchen and other supports for people in this economically depressed city. Parish minister **Josh Paweleck** works with his Manchester, Connecticut congregation in intentional ways to understand and dismantle racism and oppression within and outside of the congregation.

The stories are inspiring and too many to tell here. The good news is that these dynamic parish ministries that embrace and engage the wider communities in which they live are happening all over the United States. Wherever they are, like Cathy's quilt, they wrap their tender and vulnerable communities in love.

V. VISIONS AND
CHALLENGES AHEAD

by the Rev. Dr. Dorothy May Emerson and
the Rev. Dr. Anita Farber-Robertson

....

*While acknowledging the promise now realized since com-
munity ministry gained formal standing, the authors point
out that significant challenges to sustaining such ministries
remain. Fundamental to these challenges has been our historic commitment to congregational polity, by which we have
directed our concern and resources primarily to parish ministry. The authors recommend a number of strategies that would
help to stimulate and support community ministry, working
through congregations; beyond this, they offer several models
in which community ministries have been sustained in relationship with a congregation or a district. They specifically
call on the UUA to participate with community ministers in
creating mechanisms for financial support. They argue that
funding has remained a primary stumbling block to success.*

....

The 2005 Commission on Appraisal report, *Engaging Our Theological
Diversity*, set out to explore whether there is any common ground
across the diversity of beliefs held by today's Unitarian Universalists.
What the Commission discovered is that "what unites us far
outweighs what divides us. We are a community of faith given to
engagement with our world, using our power of the institution to
work for justice and freedom—religious or otherwise."[151] Despite

---

151 Commission on Appraisal, *Engaging Our Theological Diversity* (Boston: Unitarian Universalist
Association, 2005), 118.

differences in our understandings of how and why the world is as it is, we accept responsibility to make it a better place for ourselves and future generations, and we draw on whatever sources of religious inspiration are meaningful to us to empower our will to act.[v]

It is the thesis of this book that community ministers play an essential role in bringing that commitment to reality.

As Unitarian Universalists, we have a grand history of community ministry, one that demonstrates the power and relevance of our religious principles when they are translated into action for the sake of the world. Community ministry addresses the needs and concerns of the wider communities within which our ministers, our members, and our congregations exist as representatives of our faith. We have a theology that clearly calls us—as individuals and as congregations—to apply our values and principles to address the pressing issues of our times. We have role models, community ministers from the past and the present, who show us how to witness to our faith in particular contexts and how to act to make a real difference in the lives of those who are connected to us through "the interdependent web of all existence of which we are a part."[152] Indeed, we have rich resources with which to develop Unitarian Universalist community ministries that can help save the world.

What we do not have yet is an institutional framework that fully supports community ministry. That is not surprising in light of Rebecca Parker's observation of an unavoidable theological truth: "The realm of the religious always exceeds our efforts to contain it."[153] Just as we cannot fully capture the realm of the religious in our imaginations, neither can we fully capture the charge and claim it makes upon us in our finite, mortal institutions. Still we must try, as ever we have done, to bring our institutional life closer and more faithful to the prophetic vision of a world made fair, with all its people one.

Beginning with the earliest gatherings of community ministers, rules and structures of our congregationally based Association have been recognized as presenting certain difficulties for the advancement of community ministry. Although much has improved over the

---

152 *Engaging Our Theological Diversity*, 92.
153 Seventh UU Principle. See Principles Statement at the beginning of this book.

years, institutional systems still need to be established or adapted to nurture and support the full development of community ministry.

In November 1986, the Rev. David Cole, then Interim Director of the Benevolent Fraternity, issued the following warning at the Chapel Service held for UUA staff during the first Convocation of Community Focused Ministries:

> Martin Luther King, Jr. used to say at the Civil Rights rallies that equality for the Negro was necessary to save the souls of white folk. In like manner, Community Focus Ministry says the soul of this denomination cannot be whole unless it reaches out in care and concern to oppressed and suffering people. Until we bring all races and classes into the life of this movement, we cannot find fullness of spiritual life.[154]

If Cole is correct, in the search for fullness of spiritual life, we must ask ourselves what it would take to fully actualize the potential for community ministry within our Unitarian Universalist movement. For our spiritual health as a people of faith, we are now joining together to develop the resources necessary to make community ministry an integral part of our Association in the twenty-first century.[155] This is a partnership in which all the components of our Unitarian Universalist movement are stakeholders. It is a propitious time when we are poised to reconceive ourselves, reclaiming our place in the public square.

The world we live in is an increasingly dangerous and suffering place. In this context, our congregations offer important havens of safety and spiritual growth. It is tempting to pour the majority of our resources into our congregations. This emphasis, however, does little to change the world of suffering from which our beleaguered congregants seek refuge and toward which our congregations bear witness. We cannot protect ourselves from the world, but we can engage with that world in significant ways that will make it safer, not only for our congregations but also for all who share in the life of our

---

154 First newsletter for the Community Focused Ministry, edited by Jody Shipley, Jan. 1987, 9.

155 The large number of people who willingly contributed material or critiques to make this book possible is an example of the way in which stakeholders are identifying themselves and entering collaborative relationships in the service of strengthening and integrating community ministry into our movement.

communities and our world. It is in our self-interest, as well as the interest of all concerned, to turn our focus outward to the local communities and urban areas that are connected to our congregations.

Parish ministers and religious education professionals often have their hands full managing the day-to-day operations of the congregations they serve. Although they may be committed to community engagement, they may have little time and energy to pursue this important aspect of their ministries in any sustained way. Community ministers are ideally situated to provide leadership in developing our ministries with the wider communities of which we are a part. They can offer the guidance and experience needed to help congregations develop their engagement with this larger world.

The Commission on Appraisal, mentioned earlier, is an independent group elected by the General Assembly to review issues of concern to the UU movement, offering feedback and making recommendations to the Association. It has recognized the potential for community ministry to expand the capacity of congregations to minister "to the larger community in which it finds itself, and to the world." The Commission introduced its 1992 report, *Our Professional Ministry*, with a section called "A Vision of Ministry." This report identified the challenge of our current organizational structures: "While our congregations have consistently tried, through the UUA...the UU Service Committee, and various district and congregational programs, to minister to the larger community and to the world, our congregational polity and the concept of ministry that has gone with it have hindered our efforts." The Commission then lifted up community ministry as a solution: "The marked increase in the number of men and women who as professional ministers are going into community, rather than parish-based ministries, now offers our congregations an opportunity for a greatly enhanced prophetic ministry to the larger community and to the world."[156]

The vision and the challenge of that report call to us still, and we are responding.

---

156 Commission of Appraisal, *Our Professional Ministry: Structure, Support and Renewal* (Boston: UUA, 1992), 5.

THE CHALLENGE OF CONGREGATIONAL POLITY

Polity refers to the way an organization governs itself. To say that Unitarian Universalism is structured according to "congregational polity" means that individual congregations are self-governing and self-funded. But that's not all it means, as we learn from the historical roots of this practice. UU historian Conrad Wright points out, "Congregationalism meant, and should still mean, not the autonomy of the local church, but the community of autonomous churches."[157] Our individual congregations are part of the Unitarian Universalist Association of Congregations and its district, associate, and affiliate organizations. These ways of joining together give us far more strength than individual congregations would have by themselves.

After its study of ministry, the Commission on Appraisal began a four-year study of congregational polity, published in 1996 as *Interdependence: Renewing Congregational Polity*. The introduction includes this statement:

> We want our religious community and the network of relationships that extends beyond itself to be a living model for the good of human relationships throughout life. However, our institutional ideals and practices have lagged far behind our spiritual vision. In particular, "congregational polity" has been used as a shibboleth against the fuller recognition of our interrelationships.[158]

The report calls attention "to the paradigm shift in liberal religious thought as a whole—from independence to interdependence, from individualism to relationalism." The Commission contends "that thinking of congregational polity only as a principle of local autonomy disempowers us." Instead we need to emphasize the call to be a "community of autonomous congregations" as a source of

---

157 Conrad Wright, *Walking Together* (Boston: Skinner House, 1989).
158 Commission on Appraisal, *Interdependence: Renewing Congregational Polity* (Boston: UUA, 1996), 1.

empowerment for joint action, much more in keeping "with our spiritual vision of who we are and what we seek to become."[159]

The Commission rightly calls us back to the original meaning of congregational polity as practiced by our New England forebears. Congregational polity was designed within the context of a covenantal, associational theology. Persons gathered into congregations by voluntary association. Those congregations then were themselves gathered into covenantal associations. The autonomy was always tempered by the accountability of association. Discernment of right action and right relations was done within the context of the community and its associations. From the biblical history we traced to the Free Church tradition on American shores, the deep theology that carried us was associational. It is the secular culture of competition and individualism that has seduced us out of adhering to our most profound theological truths, and it is time now to reclaim what we have known to be true. We stand together—with each other, and ultimately with all the others who inhabit the earth.

The report went on to recommend the development of stronger lateral relationships among congregations, not just at the Association and district levels, but also among congregations that are geographically proximate or related in terms of interests and concerns. Further, the Commission called upon congregations "to be in right relation within themselves, to one another, and to other communities beyond the Association." They recommended an examination of the current Bylaws of the UUA and a process to amend them to state in positive terms "that congregational polity is not only a principle to protect local autonomy; it also affirms the interdependence of the congregations as essential to their spiritual vitality and authenticity."[160]

To enlarge the vision of the congregation, the Commission recommended understanding the role of the congregation "as the primary nexus of our spiritual life and ministry" and its central mission as "its corporate ministry (service) to the world." The purpose, then, of the UUA and other denominational organizations becomes one of enabling congregations "to carry out their ministries more effectively, both to their own constituencies...and to the world."

---

159 *Interdependence*, 171.

160 *Interdependence*, 49.

Community-based ministries are a key component in enabling congregations to carry out their ministries to the world. The Commission recognized that such ministries would be fully supported only "when congregations identify them as forms of our corporate ministry to the world, and community ministers are given professional roles within the congregations, including accountability, financial support, leading worship, and teaching."[161]

Here again, the Commission recognized the vision and the challenge of community ministry. We have congregations that often operate in isolation, with little sense of the potential they could realize if they worked together. We have community ministers who are able and willing to help congregations to work together, thereby enlarging the congregation's vision to develop corporate ministries to the world. But we have an organizational structure that does not foster the collaboration we need, since each congregation operates as a separate entity. Bridging the gap between the vision and the reality is itself a shared task. We are developing ways to collaborate between the Unitarian Universalist Association, community ministers, congregations, and a variety of organizations. The Community Ministry Summit was an example of such collaboration. Always, there is more work to be done.

EDUCATION FOR COMMUNITY MINISTRY

There are at least three important educational challenges to the development of community ministry. The first is the need to educate congregations and parish-based ministers about the importance of community ministry for them. The second is the need to develop more in-depth training for community ministers who plan to seek ordination. The third is to set up training and support for laypeople in the development of community ministries.

To help community ministry become well grounded in congregational life, congregations and parish-based ministers need to learn about the practice of community ministry and how it can enlarge

---

161 *Interdependence,* 13.

the mission and impact of congregations in the larger community. It is hoped that this book will be one step in that process. Now that ministerial education is required to enable students to develop competencies in parish, religious education, and community ministry, it becomes important that theological schools offer courses that specifically address the competency needs of community ministers.

At most seminaries, however, there is generally only one course that addresses practical matters relating to community ministry. Here is an opportunity for Unitarian Universalism to lead the way in making liberal religion manifest in the world. Many of our Unitarian Universalist ministers in training are enrolled in non-UU theological schools. To the extent that we can increase the development of community ministry consciousness and competency in the liberal religious interfaith community, we will be developing allies prepared to do the work with us.

The challenge now is to envision what theological education would include if it were designed to prepare people for community ministry. Course offerings that support and train people for community ministry and reveal to others the complexity of its challenges would serve those going into community ministry and those who will eventually interface with them.

Although this book is focused on ordained community ministry, we have an appreciation for and rejoice in recognizing one of the unique features of the community ministry movement. From the beginning it has included both lay and ordained ministers. While lay community ministry is outside of the scope of this book, we believe that Unitarian Universalist congregations and our movement in general would be enhanced by a more intentional development, recognition, and credentialing of lay community ministers. Lay community ministers have typically self-identified either their full-time work or their volunteer efforts as an outgrowth of their faith commitment.

The development of lay ministry programs in congregations has led to interest in establishing lay community ministry programs that would provide support and training for members of congregations who want to identify their volunteer efforts for justice and healing as ministry. Such programs could offer opportunities for discernment, reflection, and accountability for sustained work for social change.

They could equip people to work together to develop community ministries that involve a significant portion of the congregation. In conjunction with this, some sort of credentialing and recognition process for lay community ministers needs to be developed. We have done this with lay religious educators who share collegiality with ordained Ministers of Religious Education and with each other as lay religious educators. The Society for Community Ministries has developed a Code of Professional Practice that applies to both lay and ordained community ministers.[162] Some sort of recognition of the community ministry of the laity would surely further the movement toward a fuller living out of our principles in the world.

One of the challenges to providing the necessary education to facilitate the advancement of community ministry is determining whose responsibility it is to develop such programs. It would seem that some sort of central coordination of education for community ministry would be wise. With accessible educational resources, we could create a greatly expanded vision and mission for our faith, leading to a world healed from oppression and injustice—a world "transformed by our care."[163]

ORDINATION OF COMMUNITY MINISTERS

The ordination of ministers is symbolic of the relationship between the one who is called to ministry and those who call the ministry into being. Ordination recognizes the minister as having the calling to minister. Rev. John Gilmore explains:

> The calling of the community minister is to go out into the world and make it a better place. It is laying hold of the treasures that we have in our lives, our association, and in our congregations, and taking them out into the world to

---

162 The Code of Professional Practice developed by the Society for Community Ministries is available at www.uuscm.org.

163 Thomas Mikelson, "Wake, Now, My Senses," *Singing the Living Tradition*, #298.

apply them, so that we might help bring about a world of justice, equity and compassion.[164]

When people ordain a minister, they acknowledge this call and affirm that the person who claims it is ready to go out into the world in response. Ordination affirms the call, both for the minister and for the people who do the ordaining.

Rebecca Parker observes the reality and the challenge it presents:

As a denomination we have moved to affirm that ministries beyond the setting of the parish make sense to us. We want to recognize and support them. We have decided that we will fellowship and ordain people for such ministries....We can see that there is grounding for community ministry in our theological heritage, and in our present convictions....

But we have put ourselves at odds with our own polity. We have enacted a vision of the purpose of the church that differs from the vision embodied in our [historical New England[165] and] existing congregational polity....

In a seminar for congregations in the San Francisco Bay Area, Patti Lawrence, Dean of Students and Congregational Outreach at Starr King School, and I asked church leaders to articulate what their congregations were accomplishing of value. The consistent response was "fellowship." The church provided a sense of home, a place of safety and community. We affirmed the importance of this, but noted the absence of a sense of mission in the larger world.[166]

Parker's experience stands in stark contrast with the 2005 Commission on Appraisal Report, *Engaging Our Theological Diversity*, based on research conducted in congregations a decade after Parker's experience. The goal was to identify what it was that united Unitarian Universalists as a faith community. They concluded,

---

164 John Gilmore, "Answering the Call to Community Ministry," unpublished essay submitted for this book (2005).

165 For further discussion of historic New England roots, see "For All the Saints: Toward a Theology of Community Ministry" in this book.

166 Rebecca Parker, "A Hand Is Laid Upon Us," 1995.

We are committed to religious community as a place where we work together for a more compassionate world. It is not enough to gather in a safe, supportive sanctuary for ourselves alone. We must be visible and present to those who need us. Our experience of religious community strengthens us to go forth empowered to make a difference.[167]

We are, it appears, of two minds: one that is concerned with the well-being of the people gathered in covenanted community, and one that is concerned with the well-being of the world, our home, with which we are connected in mystery and miracle, as we often affirm in our worship. Not surprisingly the roots of this dual commitment are to be found in the history from which we have sprung and the future that we would build. Parker goes on to explain:

The basic features of New England congregationalism remain with us. It is our practice that congregations elect their own leadership. The minister is called by vote of the congregation, not appointed by any churchly authorities above and beyond the congregation. The congregation retains sole authority to ordain people to the ministry.... What is precious and unique in this tradition is its clarity that ordination belongs in the hands of the people, not in institutional power structures. This affirmation gives flesh to the belief that the spirit is at work in all people, not isolated in select religious authorities.

In brief, our historical understanding of the ordained ministry is

- *Relational*: a community ordains, and the relationship is one of trust.
- *Practical*: practical experience has shown that the work of the church flourishes when there are good leaders. The minister's work is to support and lead the life of the congregation.

---

167 *Engaging Our Theological Diversity*, 136.

- *Functional*: the holder of the ministerial office is responsible for the key functions of preaching, teaching, leading worship, administration, and pastoral care.

In the context of this polity and tradition there is no meaning to ordained ministry outside of the relationship between minister and people within the circle of the covenanted community....
In affirming community ministry, we have made a move that stretches our tradition in a way that perhaps obscures its basic integrity. The significance of the decision to fellowship and ordain community ministers must not be missed. It is a change that goes to the heart of our mission.[168]

All this is true when we understand our tradition as coming from the Unitarian roots of our faith. From the perspective of the Cambridge Platform and its inheritors, Parker rightfully recognizes that change is under way. In the context of our larger story—which includes our Universalist roots—the change can be understood as reclaiming of a part of who we were that we had inadvertently left behind. We are reminded of the immortal words of L.B. Fisher, Dean of the Chicago-based Ryder Divinity School, when he said in 1921, "Universalists are often asked to tell where they stand. The only true answer to give to this question is that we do not stand at all, we move."[169]

So it is ironic that we find ourselves caught in the tension we wove into the nature of our Association when we merged the Unitarians (the original standing-order churches) and the Universalists (who do not stand, but move)! We are now in a situation in which the dilemmas created by the historic polity we embraced from the Unitarians are finding correctives in the historic polity we inherited and archived from the Universalists. As we reclaim the wisdom and flexibilities in the Universalist polity, we continue to embrace what is known and valued in the Unitarian structure. So Parker's observation is understandable here: "In other words, we have decided (not

---

168 Rebecca Parker, "A Hand Is Laid Upon Us," 1995.
169 Charles A. Howe, *The Larger Faith* (Boston: Skinner House Books, 1993), 96.

very consciously) to operate with two different visions of the purpose of the church simultaneously."[170]

What we have developed here is a polarity—a concept in systems analysis that understands that there are certain tensions (often experienced as conflicts) built into organizations that necessarily exist and that, for the health of the organization, ought not to be resolved. These kinds of tensions or conflicts tend to move more toward one direction and then, when it seems to have gotten unbalanced too far in that direction, flow back toward the other, in a never-ending movement looping back and forth, approaching, but never fully resting at the center. In the context here, it would seem that the polarities that we have embraced are the understanding of the church as a place to gather people in for support and mutual edification, and the church as a place from which people, now strengthened and resourced, move out to serve the world. In one, meaning and the locus of divine activity is mostly in the center. In the other, meaning and the locus of divine activity is more likely found in interaction with the world.

Parker recognizes the tensions, understanding them as coming from a difference between our inherited theory and our current developing practice. She says, "They are not necessarily competing visions. But it will help if we can recognize the degree to which our basic polity and our ministerial practices have diverged."[171]

Historically, within the Unitarian form of congregational polity, the only appropriate body to ordain a minister was the congregation.[172] The Universalist tradition understood congregational polity to rest fundamentally on the associations of congregations, such as state and regional conventions, that were empowered to ordain ministers. The Universalist practice may well prove a better model for UU community ministry today, since community ministers generally serve populations beyond individual congregations.[173]

---

170 Rebecca Parker, "A Hand Is Laid Upon Us," 1995.

171 Rebecca Parker, "A Hand Is Laid Upon Us," 1995.

172 Despite the insistence on congregational ordination, there is at least one case of a Unitarian ordination at the conference level. Sarah Pratt Carr was ordained on April 21, 1896, at the Pacific Unitarian Conference, held in Lemoore, CA, according to Catherine F. Hitchings, *Universalist and Unitarian Women Ministers*, second edition (Unitarian Universalist Historical Society, 1985).

173 Stephen Schick, "Inside/Outside: A Call for Ministerial Diversity," UU Ministers Association Convocation, Hot Springs, Arkansas, March 1995; also included in the unpublished manuscript "The

Soon after the official recognition of ordained community ministry by the General Assembly in 1991, two community ministers, Cheng Imm Tan and Peter Thoms, both associates of the UU Urban Ministry, asked to be ordained jointly by the congregations making up that organization. Each congregation needed to vote separately to ordain the two ministers, and nearly half of them did. Nevertheless, several prominent ministers and congregations hotly contested the ordinations as not consistent with congregational polity. For those who chose to participate in the historic ceremony, it represented an important recognition that these two ministers were called to serve the wider community, not an individual congregation.

The way we ordain community ministers represents how we view their ministries. This broadening of ideas about who has the authority to ordain will come as we expand our awareness of our connectedness to the communities that are part of our "interdependent web."[174]

SHARED MINISTRY: CONGREGATIONS AND COMMUNITY MINISTERS

Acknowledging that community ministers have been seen "more as an adjunct than a viable part of our movement," the Commission on Appraisal's 1996 report called upon congregations to "look for ways to enhance their ministry to the wider world by becoming involved in covenantal associations with community based ministers."[175] Since 1996, rules governing community ministers have been established to require those in Preliminary Fellowship to be members of congregations and to find congregations, districts, or UUA associate organizations to "endorse" their ministries. There is, however, no parallel requirement for congregations, districts, or UUA associate organizations to enter into relationships with community ministers. Many are willing to do so, however, especially

---

Challenge of Right Relationship," 112.

174 Seventh UU Principle

175 Schick, "Inside/Outside: A Call for Ministerial Diversity," 114, 119.

when they understand how such relationships may benefit all concerned.

When they work, covenantal relationships between individual congregations and individual community ministers can be an ideal way for congregations to enlarge their ministry to the wider community. These links could be strengthened if the UUA Annual Directory included the names of community ministers along with the names of other ministers for each congregation. Likewise, the section on Professional Religious Leadership could identify the congregation or UU organization, if any, to which a community minister is linked. This would do much to heighten awareness of community ministry as a segment of our overall ministry.

There are several models of covenantal relationships that have evolved out of the needs and skills of particular community ministers and the congregations with which they are in relationship. Here we briefly share four models of effective relationships between ordained community ministers and individual Unitarian Universalist congregations.

The first model is where a community minister has a full-time job with an outside institution and shares that work with the congregation in specific ways spelled out in a covenantal agreement.

In the second model, the community minister has a part-time ministry outside the congregation and is paid on an hourly basis or receives part-time compensation for ministry within the congregation.

In a third model, the community minister is a fully compensated minister with the congregation, with a focus on facilitating the congregation's involvement in community ministry.

A fourth model involves the minister working with a small congregation part-time and pursuing community ministry in the same community in relationship with the congregation.

Affiliation with multiple congregations is yet another possibility. This arrangement, if set up with certain goals in mind, could help fulfill the promise of congregational polity to establish lateral relationships between or among congregations. There are several precedents for such projects that were in existence before community ministry was officially recognized. For instance, in the 1970s and 1980s, groups of congregations in three different parts of the country supported UU pastoral counseling services directed by UU ministers. The first was in Seattle, directed by James Zacharias (1969–81) and sponsored by the Puget Sound Council of UU Churches. Others were in New Jersey and Massachusetts.

In the social justice arena, the exemplary community ministry organization, supported by a group of congregations, is the UU Urban Ministry (UUUM), founded in the early nineteenth century as the Benevolent Fraternity of Unitarian Churches. The vision and organizational wisdom of the founders, William Ellery Channing and Joseph Tuckerman, have enabled the organization to surmount many challenges over the years. Funding for this Boston-area program comes from endowments set up years ago, annual contributions from nearly sixty member congregations, grants, and other sources, made possible via an active fund-raising program. This funding currently supports eight different programs in several locations and a professional staff that includes a community minister as executive director. Several other ordained community ministers have served as program directors; various students have worked there as interns, and some have even developed new ministries.

Member congregations of UUUM participate in annual meetings, work-days, fund-raisers, and as volunteers in various programs. Congregations that support this ministry have a consciousness that they are part of something important—something that goes beyond what any of them could do individually, carrying the vision and values of Unitarian Universalism into places where the message of healing and justice is most needed. Although efforts to replicate this model in Los Angeles and other areas have met with only limited success, there is great potential for this type of organization to have a significant impact on problems of poverty and oppression that are rampant in many of our communities and to move our congregations out of insularity and into relationship with one another.

On a smaller scale, the Rev. Jeanne Lloyd created a program in Hartford, Connecticut, that brought area congregations together to address issues of racism in their community. While in seminary, she was inspired by the Commission on Appraisal report, *Interdependence*, to conceive of a way to unite a group of congregations in pursuit of a common goal. This effort would aim to fulfill the goal and also to live out an important aspect of congregational polity: to work cooperatively in "associations of congregations." Lloyd began by inviting three UU congregations in the area to form Greater Hartford UUs Against Racism. The program began with the congregations participating in antiracism training based on the UUA's Journey Toward Wholeness program. Later the program was expanded and the name changed when an African American AME church joined the coalition. Congregations United for Racial and Economic Justice (CUREJ) sponsored a wide range of activities. Some were large, multi-church educational events, usually involving music, with choirs from the various congregations singing together. Others were smaller monthly meetings with topics or questions to explore together, the goal being to look deeply at how race affected people of different colors. Sometimes they protested together when community issues involving race occurred, like the time they stood out as witnesses against violence, after a series of shootings in West Hartford.

While the program was clearly successful and continues today, the Rev. Lloyd realized after a number of years that it was unlikely to fully support her as a community minister, even though each congregation contributed to the program from its annual budget and the project received some funding from the UUA Fund for UU Social Responsibility. In order to attract larger-scale funding, they would have needed to form a stronger central organization, and the congregations weren't ready to do that. Lloyd comments: "As long as we have no structure for incorporating community ministry into congregations and for enabling congregations to work together on joint projects, the potential for community ministry's impact will remain a great dream." [176]

EXPANDING THE VISION: COMMUNITY MINISTERS AND UU ORGANIZATIONS

Affiliation of community ministers with congregations or groups of congregations follows the Unitarian model of congregational

---

176 Jeanne Lloyd, interview with Dorothy Emerson, September 22, 2005.

polity. The Universalist model opens up the possibility of affiliation with larger bodies, such as districts or UUA associate organizations, as provided for in the policies set by the Ministerial Fellowship Committee. These two large structures of accountability are as yet largely undeveloped.

One model of district affiliation has developed in the Mountain Desert District, which includes Montana, Wyoming, Colorado, Utah, New Mexico, and parts of Idaho and Texas. When he first moved to the district in 1988, the Rev. James Zacharias began meeting with district executive Sue Turner to explore the possibilities of connecting his ministry of pastoral counseling with the district. He had previously served for twelve years as director of the Unitarian Counseling Service in the Seattle area. A community-ministry committee was formed and policies and procedures were established, leading to an arrangement whereby he became recognized as a community minister affiliated with the district. In this role he organized meetings with other community ministers in the region and helped strengthen the process for district affiliation. A key component of the resulting arrangement is an annual peer-review process that he developed. The minister responds in writing to a series of questions about personal, professional, and spiritual life, and then meets for several hours with a committee that includes a parish minister and colleagues in the minister's field.[177]

Community minister Nadine Swahnberg describes the peer review process as grueling but mind-expanding: "We do it because we believe it helps us, helps our ministries, strengthens communications, and helps us to get the word out about what we do and why we do it." [178] In addition to providing a record of ongoing community ministry work and its connection with the district, peer review brings accountability to these ministries. Each year at district annual meetings, a brochure describing the various community ministries in the district is provided for each congregation, and periodically workshops on community ministry are offered.

District programs can expand the potential for community ministry to have visibility and usefulness to all their congregations.

---

177 Jim Zacharias, interview with Dorothy Emerson, September 12, 2005.

178 Nadine Swahnberg, e-mail to Dorothy Emerson, September 14, 2005.

Districts can educate their member congregations about community ministry and can provide assistance in setting up relationships between congregations and individual ministers. In most districts there are far more congregations than community ministers, so district programs can enable congregations that would like to utilize the services of community ministers to find them.

Affiliation of community ministers with UUA associate member organizations, although possible since the early 1990s, has only recently begun to take concrete form. In 2007 the Rev. Jade Angelica and the Rev. Dorothy Emerson established covenants with the Unitarian Universalist Women's Federation as affiliate ministers. The UU United Nations Office established a policy for affiliating community ministers. The UU Service Committee, the third such organization, has had community ministers as staff members and has received funding from the UUA to sponsor a ministerial intern who has the intent to practice as a community minister. The models that emerge from such relationships offer new ways for community ministries to engage with the larger UU movement.

To properly ground existing and emerging community ministries in congregational life, systems need to be established to facilitate relationships and covenants that maximize the talents, energies, and resources of all participants. Guidelines need to be created to help congregations and ministers negotiate effective agreements, with mutually advantageous benefits. In the meantime, UUA district and associate organizations can be of great assistance in facilitating the process of connecting community ministers with congregations. With such support, community ministry can begin, as Pacific Southwest District Executive Ken Brown suggests, "to break down walls and extend our Unitarian Universalist love and compassion into the non-UU world." [179] Community minister Kay Jorgensen offers this vision: "I see districts being able to offer to fellowships and small churches a way of participating in this kind of energy—small churches that can't do it alone, but together they can."[180]

---

179 Ken Brown, e-mail to Jody Shipley, August 27, 1998.
180 Kay Jorgensen, interview with Mary Ganz, August 25, 2005.

FUNDING FOR COMMUNITY MINISTRY

Money is *the* big stumbling block for many people in imagining how an enlarged vision of Unitarian Universalism that fully incorporates community ministry could be actualized. Clearly this is a topic that challenges us—as individuals, as congregations, and as an Association. There are no easy answers, but there is hope.

First of all, it is important for us to discuss money in relationship to community ministry. For too long community ministers, especially those not employed by outside agencies, have struggled financially. In their passion for their ministries, some community ministers have volunteered to do important work without compensation or for small stipends. They have funded their community ministries by tapping family savings or by being dependent on their partners. They have supported their ministries through other jobs, such as housecleaning, construction, computer work, or even parish ministry. They have cobbled together bits and pieces of funding from a variety of sources to support the work they are called to do. Among the shining stars in the community ministry movement are those who have barely made it financially and who have risked poverty in retirement after a career dedicated to Unitarian Universalist community ministry.

Until now, much of the funding for the organizational development of UU community ministry has come from grants provided by UU sources. In the mid-1980s, grants supported the first gatherings of Extra-Parochial Clergy and Community Focused Ministers before the two groups joined to form the Society for the Larger Ministry (SLM). During the first four years of the organization, SLM received five different grants to support conferences and steering committee meetings. Without this funding, it is doubtful that many community ministers would have been able to attend. From 1986 to 2006, the UU Funding Program contributed over $130,000, in nineteen separate grants, to the development of UU community ministry. This funding provided support for four different community ministry organizations, including one district community ministry council.[181]

---

181 The four organizations are Society for the Larger Ministry (now called Society for Community Ministries) and its predecessor organizations, Extra-Parochial Clergy and Community-Focused Ministries; UU Community Ministry Center; Community Ministry Coalition; and Pacific Central District Community Ministry Council.

These groups utilized this funding for organizational development, gatherings of community ministers, educational materials, and special projects to develop models for community ministry. Many more grants have been given to support community ministry programs in individual congregations and local area community ministry organizations. The UU Ministers Association provided periodic support for community ministry projects and included support for the Community Ministry Focus Group in its regular budget for several years. The largest funder, the Unitarian Universalist Veatch Program at Shelter Rock, granted $295,000 over seven years to the Urban Disciples program.[182] This adds up to an institutional investment of over $450,000, entirely in the form of grants.

While grant funding certainly is significant, it is not dependable and offers no base of consistency and sustainability upon which ongoing programs and ministries can be built. Permanent line items in budgets of congregations, districts, and the UUA are more consistent with building a viable and sustainable infrastructure. For the first time, in the 2006 budget of the UUA, a small line item was designated for community ministry and the newly formed Professional Leadership Coordinating Council.[183] A two-year, part-time internship within the Ministry and Professional Leadership staff group has been funded in 2008 and 2009 to study the current state of community ministry in our movement, assess needs, and help begin to create a vision for the future. The process of institutionalizing community ministry has begun.

Over the years, various groups of community ministers and consultations on community ministry identified UUA staff support as essential for the full development of community ministry. One of the hopes has been that the UUA would provide settlement services, which might include both helping community ministers find positions and helping congregations and community ministers make connections with each other. However, as Ralph Mero explained,

---

182 Framed initially as an urban rather than community ministry, this program has enabled a number of community ministries to develop, by supporting social justice work in urban congregations and assisting the people who direct such work.

183 The Professional Leadership Coordinating Council, formed in 2005, is composed of representatives from the UU Ministers Association, LREDA (representing religious educators), Society for Community Ministries, UU Musicians Network, and Association of UU Administrators. Its purpose is to foster collegial relationships among professional staff in congregations and to address common concerns.

"The Association never had the money to establish a job referral program...for community ministers similar to settlement for parish ministers and [ministers of religious education], and thus our community ministers have had to find ways to earn a living as a minister largely through non-parish entities on their own."[184]

If community ministry is to thrive and grow to fulfill its potential, we must determine how to fund it adequately. Fortunately there are resources both within and beyond our congregations. As congregations and individual members learn more about community ministry, there is no doubt they will want to be part of supporting programs that further their values and principles. Success stories like those in this book, the development of district community ministry structures, and growing support and visibility throughout the UU movement will help community ministry move forward toward increasing its potential. And new sources of funding are emerging.

For instance, with the curtailing of welfare and other government support programs since the mid-1990s, there has been increasing reliance nationwide on faith-based initiatives. Although we may decry the elimination of government programs for those in greatest need, the reality is that public funding is now available for programs operated by Unitarian Universalist congregations and organizations. However, we need to prepare ourselves by developing more sophisticated organizational systems to qualify for and implement large programs that bring justice and healing—not just charity—to our communities.

The potential for philanthropic donations to benefit UU community ministries is growing. According to the Boston College Social Welfare Research Institute, an estimated $41 trillion in wealth is being transferred from the World War II generation to Baby Boomers in the first half of the twenty-first century.[185] Leaders in the field of philanthropy predict that a significant portion of this wealth will be used for philanthropic purposes that support values of caring and social betterment. Well-managed community ministry programs

---

184 Ralph Mero, e-mail to Dorothy Emerson, September 16, 2005. Mero served as director of the Office of Church Staff Finance and is fellowshipped as a community minister.

185 John J. Havens and Paul G. Schervish, "Why the $41 Trillion Wealth Transfer Is Still Valid: A Review of Challenges and Questions," *The Journal of Gift Planning*, 7: 1st Quarter 2003, 11–15, 47–50.

that touch people's lives and transform communities may well attract some of this wealth.

Before we can become eligible for large-scale funding from either public or private sources, we must first decide that it is within the mission of our congregations and our Association to respond to the call to community. We must then develop infrastructures that can administer large projects to address specific needs and concerns over the long haul. Such work has the potential to transform individual lives and communities and bring justice and healing to our broken world. To take it on, however, we need to be willing to commit to long-term engagement and change. We would do well to consider the words of Nelson Mandela to the people of South Africa: "Our deepest fear is not that we are inadequate. Our deepest fear is that we are powerful beyond measure."[186]

To acknowledge our power is to begin the long journey to accountability. It is demanding, arduous, and uncertain. We will inevitably fall short. But the rewards of this long walk are the reasons why we have come together—searching for truth, meaning, and the assurance that we matter, that we are a part of something bigger than ourselves, and that our lives make a difference.

CREATING COMMUNITIES OF ACCOUNTABILITY AND SUPPORT

As we have seen, community ministers have often labored alone, experiencing an isolation that undermined them and craving the faith connections with Unitarian Universalism we are trying to nurture. As ordained community ministry has developed, one concern that has been regularly voiced is that these ministers who are working publicly in the name of Unitarian Universalism need to be accountable to our faith. What follows are examples of two programs that provide models for the kind of support that can significantly help in the development of a community ministry.

---

186 Marianne Williamson, *Return to Love* (Harper-Collins, 1992), passage quoted by Nelson Mandela in his inaugural speech, May 10, 1994.

Deborah Holder, past-president of the UU Society for Community Ministries, described the primary challenge facing community ministers, especially those involved in social justice work: "Nurturing and sustaining a communal process for establishing right relations within the congregation and supporting the congregation as it begins to move out into right relations with the surrounding community is sometimes daunting and always risky."[187] Yet this is what we need to do to put our faith into action in the communities beyond the walls of our congregations. Community ministers, in turn, often need some kind of larger group with whom to regularly engage in reflection and analysis as they participate in this daunting and risky work.

Faithful Fools Street Ministry,[188] one of the few group community ministry programs in existence, developed one such support program. Because Faithful Fools has a facility with meeting space, full-time staff, and a well-developed program, it has frequently served as an internship site for ministry students in the San Francisco area, where it is located. Over the years many students and already-ordained ministers have worked with Faithful Fools. Some were preparing for community ministry but ended up taking parish ministry positions; others were parish ministers moving into community ministry. Fools minister Kay Jorgensen recognized that the distinctions between parish and community ministries is not clear-cut—that ministers are often in a constant state of discernment. She explained: "We're never quite done as ministers. We are still creating and keeping our ministries alive. This keeps us humble."[189]

To help people move through the process of discernment with consciousness and support, the Fools initiated the New Ministry Incubator Project and sought funding from the Fund for Unitarian Universalism. The funding they received helped them develop and extend their internship program and support ministers who were working to create ministries authentic to their sense of call. The Rev. Jorgensen explained the goal as helping people to "find a dimension of ministry that is already within them and bring it to legitimate expression."

While this program was funded for only one year, it showed the importance of providing communities of support for exploring the

---

187 Deborah Holder, in *Urban Discipleship*, 6.
188 Read more about Faithful Fools in the "Community Ministries Made Real" section of this book.
189 Kay Jorgensen, interview with Dorothy Emerson, September 21, 2005.

deep questions that arise in the process of creating and re-creating community ministries. Even without funding, the Incubator Project continued through monthly conference calls. These calls supported people going out in the world to do their ministries, providing an opportunity for them to check in with others about their work and encouraging them to follow their vision.

The much larger program, Urban Disciples, was funded for seven years by the Unitarian Universalist Veatch Program at Shelter Rock. This funding provided direct support for social justice programs in urban congregations, paid for a consultant to coordinate the program, and made it possible for the Disciples to come together for twice-yearly meetings. When Kate Lore joined the program and attended her first gathering, she was initially irritated by the interactive pace, coming as she was from a very task-oriented perspective.[190] Deborah Holder, who served as program consultant, explained that what developed through these gatherings was "a new learning organization in which people at all levels, individually and collectively, are continually increasing their capacity to act and produce results they really care about."[191] Lore and the others came to truly value the opportunity these gatherings provided for theological development, social analysis, and solidarity with others working in urban ministries.

What has been learned from these two programs is that community ministers and ministries in formation benefit greatly from ongoing support and relationships with other community ministers. Such groups provide emotional connection, perspective, and information crucial to developing and sustaining community ministries. Individual community ministers need this support to fulfill their purposes. Deborah Holder explained how important this support was to the success of the individual Urban Disciples programs:

When the winds whip up, the reciprocal gift the Urban Disciples share is a networked community of peer support. In addition to implementing goals established by each congregation, the project's aspiration since inception is group cultivation of a professional field of love and trust that

---

190 Kate Lore, interview with Dorothy Emerson.
191 In *Urban Discipleship,* 6.

allows these disparate members of religious communities and their constituencies across the country to bring their best selves to the work of social transformation.[192]

People who have been interviewed for this book have confirmed that what is needed for community ministry to grow and thrive is a structure of support, perhaps based on models like the Incubator Project and Urban Disciples. Parish minister Bill Hamilton-Holway envisioned the evolution of new ways "to support the emergence of community ministries and keep them in the family," perhaps through the creation of a large, well-funded program to provide training and peer support for community ministers.[193] This program might include assistance in creating appropriate internships, specific educational opportunities for community ministry not currently offered in theological schools, supervision and resources, and facilitation of placement in congregations and other organizations.[194] Others suggested that such a program might provide a place of affiliation for those for whom congregational or other organizational affiliation is not appropriate. Some kind of support structure is needed, especially in this formative period, to provide crucial next steps that would enable community ministry to fulfill its promise. This promise is nothing less than the transformation of Unitarian Universalism and the unleashing of our moral imagination to confront and heal the despair and brokenness of the world in which we live.[195]

FROM VISION TO REALITY: CREATING COMMUNITY MINISTRIES

There are many resources available to help community ministers, congregations, and other organizations overcome our reluctance to turn the vision of community ministry into reality. We can learn

---

192 *Urban Discipleship*, 6.

193 Bill Hamilton-Holway, e-mail to Dorothy Emerson, September 17, 2005.

194 Bill Hamilton-Holway, interview with Dorothy Emerson, Berkeley, CA, May 12, 2005.

195 In *Urban Discipleship*, 29.

from the models in our own UU experience, past and present. We can also learn from community ministries developed by other faith-based institutions. Carl Dudley, who directed major multi-faith research projects studying congregational life and community ministries,[196] has compiled a valuable resource resulting from these studies: *Community Ministry: New Challenges, Proven Steps to Faith-Based Initiatives*. James P. Wind, president of the Alban Institute, recommends it:

> Here are steps to help congregations develop new community ministries—and actual instruments and processes that can be used to help congregations make the move from vague intentions to specific actions. Here are examples of various types of social ministry and testimonies from people who have shaped them.[197]

Key steps in the process are carefully laid out:

- establishing your particular ministry
- determining community needs and how these needs intersect with the talents and interests of the congregation
- engaging with community leaders as well as people the ministry might serve to determine the best ways to shape the ministry
- raising money and hiring staff
- developing partnerships with other groups involved in similar work
- integrating the community ministry purpose with the congregation's mission
- designing a process to encourage and sustain the spiritual growth of the leaders and participants in the ministry.[198]

---

196 The studies took place at McCormick and Hartford Seminaries.

197 In Carl S. Dudley, *Community Ministry: New Challenges, Proven Steps to Faith-Based Initiatives* (Bethesda, MD: The Alban Institute, 2002), xi. The Alban Institute is an ecumenical, interfaith organization founded in 1974, which supports congregations through book-publishing, educational seminars, consulting services, and research.

198 Dudley, 138–174.

With Theodore Parker we believe that the "arc of the moral universe" is long, but it ultimately "bends toward justice," and we, ministers and congregants, work to make it so. Bending the arc of the universe toward justice is what we do when we participate in community ministries. It is a limitless vision, as Kay Jorgensen, community minister in San Francisco, makes clear:

> We are as great an association of Unitarian Universalist churches as the number of ministers who can carry our message into the world and carry the world's message back into our congregations. We can help bring the change we talk about, without thinking in terms of numbers of members all the time. We can have some kind of natural growth by keeping our doors open and helping community ministers carry our message from church to world and from world back to church.[199]

The Rev. Diane Miller offered an intriguing question. She wondered what would happen if, instead of talking about how to get more people into our churches, we paid more attention to opening the doors of the church and letting people out. We need better ways of sending people forth to do the work of the church in the larger world.[200]

EMBRACING THE VISION OF COMMUNITY MINISTRY

Throughout the history of Unitarian Universalism, the call to community has been issued over and over again. As this exploration of community ministry concludes, we turn to some of the voices that have challenged us to hear and respond to that call.

In 1969, the Rev. George K. Beach wrote an article on "New Ministries" for the *Journal of the Liberal Ministry*, calling for the

199 Kay Jorgensen, interview with Mary Ganz, August 25, 2005.
200 Diane Miller, interview with Dorothy Emerson, October 20, 2005.

church to "become more fully engaged in the life of the surrounding community, to the end of becoming more fully responsible for the life and life-conditions of its neighbors." He explained the central importance of ministry to the larger community as "a basic function of the church, but one we have barely learned how to carry out under the conditions of contemporary metropolitan life." He named four elements that are now understood as basic building blocks for community ministry: development of "a ministry of the laity, a plurality of specialized ministries, new forms of the congregation, and new forms of inter-congregational cooperation."[201]

This book has provided flesh to these four elements, identifying ways in which each can be more fully developed.

In 1988 at the second annual gathering of the Society for the Larger Ministry, the Rev. Jody Shipley declared to the congregation gathered for Sunday morning worship at the First Unitarian Church of Chicago:

Community ministry is changing the face of our Association. Not that it is new, not that it is small, quite the contrary. It is old and it is common among us. It is changing the thinking of UUs because it is calling from outside the familiar boundaries of policy and process and congregation and is challenging Unitarian Universalism to embrace the vision that we declare in our principles and purposes.

Shipley continued:

There is a spirit moving through us. By "us" I mean we Unitarian Universalists. It is deep and it is hungry. There is a spirit that is calling us to declare our mission. We know in our hearts that this will mean deep change and deep commitment, and that churches and fellowships will no longer be just a haven, but that we were meant to do something in this world that will make a difference.[202]

---

201 George K. Beach, "New Ministries," *Journal of the Liberal Ministry* 9 (Spring 1969), 53.

202 Jody Shipley, "Community Ministry in Our Midst," sermon given together with David Arksey and Carolyn McDade, First Unitarian Church, Chicago, Nov. 13, 1988.

Jody Shipley offered prophetic words as one outside, speaking truth to the power structure of the UUA. We think of her in the prophetic tradition. But as we remember our biblical roots, the prophetic tradition included those inside the palace walls as well, prophets such as Nathan, who spoke truth to King Solomon. We have had our in-house prophets too.

In 1991, the Rev. David Pohl, then Director of the UUA Department of Ministry, shared his hopes with those attending the Society for the Larger Ministry annual conference in Cambridge, Massachusetts. His hopes are our hopes. We hope they are yours.

My hope is that community ministries will help all of us become more committed to the world beyond the local parish, more committed to one of justice and community.

My hope is that community ministries will be...seen, valued, and supported, even mandated, by the principles of our faith. To be liberal is to be open, inquiring, generous. To be religious is to bind ourselves to one another, to cultivate the connections that affirm our humanness. Community ministry can only strengthen such openness, outreach and connectedness....

It is my hope that there will be a *mutual* reaching out of community ministers and local congregations toward each other....

It is my hope that the Association itself will explore ways to help fund some community ministries.... It is not a polity problem but one that has to do with imagination, organizational will, and the gentle art of persuasion.

The challenge for the Association is to take your ministries seriously. We need to develop significant support services, establish clear standards and training opportunities for the various specialties, and explore funding prospects and the generating of congregational and Associational positions that do not presently exist.[203]

We have made progress. Many of these hopes are being realized, or the steps to bring them closer to fruition are under way. It has been the work of all the saints, not just a few. Together we can continue. We can make this the time in which community ministry will reach its potential to bring healing and justice to the world. The world needs our liberating ministries, and we need to be engaged in creating a world "transformed by our care."

---

203 David Pohl, Society for the Larger Ministry annual conference, Cambridge, Massachusetts, Nov. 1991.

ABOUT THE AUTHORS

Dorothy May Emerson

The Rev. Dr. Dorothy May Emerson, retired Unitarian Universalist minister, served in parish, religious education, and community ministries for twenty-five years, primarily in Massachusetts. Her passion for community ministry began in seminary when she attended the Convocation on Community Focused Ministries in 1986 and continued parallel to her parish ministry in her role as founder-director of the UU Women's Heritage Society. She is the author-editor of *Standing Before Us: Unitarian Universalist Women and Social Reform, 1776–1936* (Skinner House, 2000); editor of *Glorious Women: Award-Winning Sermons about Women* (2004); and cocreator of *Becoming Women of Wisdom: Marking the Passage into the Crone Years* (2009). She and her spouse, Donna Clifford, formed Rainbow Solutions in 1998 to help people and organizations move toward greater social and environmental responsibility in their investments and their lives. Dorothy is currently writing a book about the 1960s.

Anita Farber-Robertson

The Rev. Dr. Anita Farber-Robertson served as settled minister for the First Parish in Canton, Massachusetts from 1980 to 1991, during which time she also began teaching at Andover Newton Theological School. She served the Unitarian Universalist Church of Greater Lynn from 1991 until 1999, at which time she became an adjunct Professor of Communication at Andover Newton Theological School, which led to her becoming credentialed as a Community Minister. In 2001 she accepted the invitation to become the Interim Minister at the First Universalist Society of Rockport, Massachusetts, and began the journey of Accredited

Interim Ministry, which continues to be her love and calling. She is also available to congregations through Learning Edge Consulting. She is the author of *Learning While Leading: Increasing Your Effectiveness in Ministry*, published by Alban Institute.

Mary McKinnon Ganz

The Rev. Mary Ganz grew up in Quincy, Illinois, and lived half her life in the San Francisco Bay Area. Prior to seminary at Pacific School of Religion, she was a news reporter for the Associated Press, and a reporter and editor at the *San Francisco Examiner*, where she covered the AIDS epidemic. Her passion in ministry is creating transformative worship, inspiring conversations of depth and connection, and preaching a countercultural ethic of Beloved Community. Mary and her spouse JD Benson served in San Francisco at the Faithful Fools Street Ministry and continue to be inspired by the mission of the Faithful Fools to see the "light, courage, intelligence, strength and creativity of [everyone] we encounter." They have served since 2010 as senior co-ministers of First Parish UU in Brewster, Massachusetts.

Kathleen R. Parker

Dr. Kathleen Parker is a Unitarian Universalist historian, writer, and editor living in Pittsburgh, Pennsylvania. She serves on the board of the Unitarian Universalist History and Heritage Society and is the current editor of the *Journal of Unitarian Universalist History*. She is a lay leader and board member at the First Unitarian Church of Pittsburgh, and is author of *Sacred Service in Civic Space: Three Hundred Years of Community Ministry in Unitarian Universalism* (2007), and *Here We Have Gathered: The Story of Unitarian Universalism in Western Pennsylvania, 1808–2008* (2010).

Rebecca Ann Parker

The Rev. Dr. Rebecca Parker, President and Professor of Theology at Starr King School for the Ministry, is co-author of *Saving Paradise: How Christianity Traded Love of This World for Crucifixion and Empire* (Beacon Press, 2008; Canterbury Press, 2012) and *A House for Hope: The Promise of Progressive Religion for the Twenty-First Century* (Beacon Press, 2010).

INDEX